Science for non-scientists

AN EXAMINATION OF OBJECTIVES
AND CONSTRAINTS IN THE
PRESENTATION OF SCIENCE TO
NON-SPECIALISTS

J. S. R. GOODLAD

OXFORD UNIVERSITY PRESS

1973

Oxford University Press, Ely House, London W.1

GLASGOW NEW YORK TORONTO MELBOURNE WELLINGTON
CAPE TOWN IBADAN NAIROBI DAR ES SALAAM LUSAKA ADDIS ABABA
DELHI BOMBAY CALCUTTA MADRAS KARACHI LAHORE DACCA
KUALA LUMPUR SINGAPORE HONG KONG TOKYO

PRINTED IN GREAT BRITAIN
BY RICHARD CLAY (THE CHAUCER PRESS), LTD.,
BUNGAY, SUFFOLK

Preface

THIS study was instigated by the late Lord Jackson of Burnley, Pro-Rector of Imperial College, who, as member of both the Dainton Committee and the Swann Committee, was interested in the form and content of scientific and technological education. At Imperial College, he expressed this interest through enthusiastic support for studies in the humanities and social sciences designed to enrich the education of engineers. He was equally interested in the provision of science in the university education of arts students who might ultimately find their way into government or science-based industries. He therefore suggested a study of the matter and was instrumental in obtaining funds from the Leverhulme Trust and Guinness Awards for this purpose.

As is argued in this book, the science education of arts students at university is part of the much wider question of the access of the non-specialist to science culture. There is relatively little activity at British universities which is specifically designed to introduce science into the education of arts students. This book explores the reasons for this and in so doing broadens the field of inquiry considerably.

Through the munificence of the Leverhulme Trust and Guinness Awards, I had the benefit of the assistance at various times and in various ways of Mrs. J. Freeman, Mr. K. du Toit, Mrs. S. Segal, and Miss V. M. Taylor. They gathered a large amount of information about the dissemination of science in education and elsewhere. Paul Briscoe, Allun Jones, and Martin Tobias also gave some help in the early stages of the inquiry. I am sorry that in the interests of economy and coherence I have been able to use only a fraction of the material they collected. As the study progressed, certain objectives of science education for non-specialists seemed to emerge as being the most important ones; similarly, the constraints discussed in this book seemed to be crucial. I hope, therefore, that my concentration on certain selected sectors of educational activity up to and including the university gives some indication of the problems faced by those who wish to see science an integral part of the general culture—and, therefore, part of the intellectual background of those who administer particular scientific activities in government, industry, or elsewhere, and of those who are interested in science as practitioners or as commentators.

As the greater part of the book deals with science in education, I hope it will be of interest to educators: not only scientists, but more importantly non-scientists, of whom I am one. Indeed, I consider the fact that I am not a scientist to be one of my principal qualifications in writing a book of this kind. Although I have worked among scientists and engineers for ten years now, at the Massachusetts Institute of Technology and at Imperial College, and have therefore seen at close quarters something of what they do, my own science education stopped at G.C.E. A-level. I therefore approach the question of science in general culture with what I hope is the mixture of interest and cynicism, fear and delight, of the non-specialist. I hope that the question 'Science for What?' will strike a chord in the minds of readers other than those professionally engaged with science. The air these days is thick with vogue-words—pollution, environment, conservation, and so on—and non-scientists may feel at a disadvantage in much current debate. For reasons I give in the book, I do not think that they need be at a disadvantage. And I hope that my discussion of science in education will also be of value to parents with children trying to decide whether to go on the 'arts side' or on the 'science side' at school. The decision does not have to be 'either–or'—and the more people that realize this, the less frequently will the decision be represented as such.

J.S.R.G.

Imperial College of Science and Technology
London, SW7
1971

Acknowledgements

I AM grateful to the many people in schools, polytechnics, universities, examining boards, and other institutions and organizations who answered the questions of myself and my assistants. In particular, we received most valuable help and advice from: Mr. Austen Albu, M.P.; Miss G. Allen, Froebel College; Mr. John Baker, Leicester University; Dr. A. A. Bath, Association of Commonwealth Universities; Mr. G. S. Bosworth, formerly of English Electric Ltd.; Dr. J. K. Brierley, H.M.I.; Mr. M. G. Brown, Sussex University; Mr. Nigel Calder; Dr. Cornelius Casey, who kindly lent me his thesis; Dr. A. Clow, B.B.C.; Mr. G. Cunliffe, University of Bristol; Professor Sir Frederick Dainton, University of Oxford; Mr. J. C. Dancy, Master of Marlborough College; Dr. Duncan Davies, I.C.I. Ltd., Professor J. T. Davies, Birmingham University; Mr. A. M. Duncan, Loughborough University; Dr. D. O. Edge, Edinburgh University; Professor H. L. Elvin, London University; Mr. J. F. Embling, Department of Education and Science; Mr. R. J. Silvey, Mr. B. P. Emmett, and Miss M. Withers, B.B.C. Audience Research Department; Mr. L. F. Ennever, Nuffield Foundation; Dr. H. M. Finniston, British Steel Corporation; Mr. H. G. Frost, London University; Mr. Maurice Goldsmith, Director of the Science of Science Foundation; Mr. F. Greenaway, Science Museum, London; Mr. Brian Groombridge, Independent Television Authority; Mr. G. Hall, B.B.C.; Mr. M. Hall, Industrial Manpower Project, London School of Economics; Professor A. R. Hall, Imperial College; Professor H. F. Halliwell, University of East Anglia; Dr. A. H. Halsey, Oxford University; Mr. G. B. Harrison, Director of the Schools Council Technology in Schools Project; Mr. S. W. Hockey, Southampton University; Professor M. E. Howard, formerly of London University; Mr. D. Hutchings, Oxford University; Mr. N. Coulton, Mr. A. H.

Iliffe, and Professor D. J. E. Ingram, Keele University; Professor F. R. Jevons, Manchester University; Mr. D. Layton, Leeds University; Mr. J. Maddox, Editor of *Nature*; Sir David Martin, the Royal Society; Dr. J. Mitchell, Social Science Research Council; Mr. S. Moore-Coulson, Confederation of British Industry; Mr. M. C. McCarthy, I.C.I. Ltd.; Mr. J. McCloy, B.B.C.; Miss M. D. McCreath, Essex University; Dr. F. McKim, Marlborough College; Mr. F. T. Naylor, Schools Council; Mr. D. E. Newbold, Henbury School Bristol, who kindly lent me his thesis; Professor W. R. Niblett, London University; Professor R. A. C. Oliver, Manchester University; Mr. S. P. Osmond, the Treasury; Professor A. D. C. Peterson, Oxford University; Dr. W. G. Potter, Science Research Council; Mr. J. Raven and Miss R. Morton-Williams, Government Social Survey; Dr. J. J. Ravetz, Leeds University; Mr. J. M. Robertson, British Association for the Advancement of Science; Mr. N. Scott, Nottingham University; Mr. R. Sibson, Schools Council; Mr. R. Irvine Smith, York University; Mr. G. J. Spence, Department of Education and Science; Mr. R. Stevens, British Association for the Advancement of Science; Mr. W. Tapper, General Secretary of the Association for Science Education; the late Dr. Gerald Walters, Bath University; Mr. T. R. Weaver, Department of Education and Science; Mr. J. Weston, the Royal Institution.

Contents

x   *Contents*

Introduction

T HIS book is about the transmission of culture. It discusses ways in which lay people can become involved with one element of general culture—science—and the constraints which are faced by those seeking to make science part of general culture.

Culture is defined here as the reaction to and handling of their environment by groups of people. The definition implies that culture is not 'top dressing', not the life-style of a leisured and wealthy élite, but that part of a community's way of life which can be described and transmitted from one generation to another. Clearly, technology is already part of our way of life: science, however, is not. The housewife who flicks switches on a complicated washing-machine or her husband to whom a car is his second skin may still react to scientific explanation of the physical principles through which their devices work with the hoary phrase 'Don't blind me with science!'

It may, or may not, be important for the ordinary citizen to be 'blinded with science'; but large sums of money are devoted to science, and inventions and discoveries have an unprecedented potential for altering the life of the community (the 'general culture') for better or worse. The direction of scientific enterprise is increasingly less dependent on the independent insights of 'men of genius' and is more and more controlled by bureaucracies, which operate in a 'climate of opinion'. And the 'climate of opinion' is, in turn, influenced by the questions which are asked in public.

Political commentators do not hesitate to question and comment upon highly complicated economic questions, matters of public morals, and the like. But often the activities of scientists are regarded as inscrutable mysteries, not open to the questionings of those uninformed in the specialisms involved. This is an unnecessary, if not undesirable, state of affairs, as this book seeks to show. It is not necessary to know all the technical details of *how* a piece of scientific work is carried out to be able to ask the crucial question: *why* is it being carried out at all? But a certain degree of confidence is required for the 'layman' to ask *why*; and this confidence is likely to come from some exposure to the purposes and practices of science.

The questioning of the scientific enterprise by intelligent laymen is probably more important than ever before. Lord (then Sir Solly) Zuckerman (1970, p. 107) has commented that the figure of annual expenditure on scientific research and development in the United Kingdom is now over £1000 million. Indeed, in 1968–9, expenditure was over £1016 million (Central Statistical Office 1971, p. 154, Table 164). Which is to say that something between £10 and £20 is being spent on research and development each year for every man, woman, and child in these islands. Zuckerman has estimated that the working population of scientists and engineers is now about 350 000. This is a high level of activity, and one that merits public interest.

No less daunting is the increasing flood of scientific literature. Writing on the storage and retrieval of scientific information D. J. Urquhart (1970, p. 519), Director of the National Lending Library for Science and Technology, has described how the output of scientific literature in the next fifteen years is likely to equal the previous output in the whole history of mankind. In one week, the National Lending Library receives about 8000 separate items containing probably more than a million pages in perhaps fifty languages. Not surprisingly, Urquhart concluded that, as the mountains of the records of man's achievements grow higher, it is going to be easier to add to these piles than to decide what to do with them. Are these mountains of information to become Himalayas of the Mind, accessible only to the select few? It ought hardly to be so, for science is deeply embedded in the life of the community at many points; so much so that it is often difficult, if not pointless, to try to distinguish science from technology, or technology from any other social activity.

Science has become an important part of the policy of governments: and, in a democracy, the policy of governments is everybody's business. To take but one example: in *Science and the policies of governments*, a committee of the Organization for Economic Co-operation and Development (O.E.C.D. 1963) has spelled out some of the implications of science for government policies. In matters of economic policy it is important to know what constitutes a return for investment in science, particularly in basic or fundamental research which cannot be planned according to conventional economic criteria but which should, nevertheless, command some funds. Social problems (urban living, health, communication, etc.) involve a host of questions not only in the social sciences but also in the physical sciences. Military policy is increasingly dependent upon science and technology. Foreign policy, apart from its military aspects, can also be strongly influenced by considerations of national prestige, which are highly sensitive to achievements in science and technology. Aid programmes rely to an increasing extent on scientific expertise. And, of course, education and manpower policies are intimately concerned with what science should be taught to whom and why.

These are all matters of common concern, not necessarily subject only to the judgements of experts. Yet the situation highlighted in Lord Snow's famous Rede Lecture of 1959, and reviewed by him in *The two cultures and a second look* (1964), still persists: namely, that persons educated with the greatest intensity we know can no longer communicate with each other on the plane of their major intellectual concern (op. cit., p. 60). The matter is of such fundamental importance that no excuse is needed for trying to diagnose the constraints operating on those who wish to see general culture suffused with science.

The question is not one of simply being well informed, though this is important. Snow originally proposed the second law of thermodynamics as a fundamental item of the intellectual equipment of the modern man who sought to 'understand' science. In his *Second Look* (1964), he tentatively substituted molecular biology (pp. 73f.) because, although of less theoretical comprehensiveness, this branch of science is likely to affect the way men think of themselves more profoundly than any scientific advance since Darwin. Information of this sort is of the essence of modern 'humanist' culture. For, if people are not to be reduced to pawns in a game played by élites, the main justification for any cultural manipulation should be to increase their self-awareness—their knowledge of their relation to their physical and social environment and their powers of control of it—which, in turn, should lead to self-confidence, self-control, freedom from irrational and unnecessary fears, and so on. In this respect, information as such is only a means to an end: the end being the cultural confidence to ask questions and to have some idea of what constitutes a satisfactory answer.

There are many ways in which cultural values are transmitted, but by far the most important is education, which is the main subject of this book. Some people (a group treated at length in this book) spend their first 21 years, almost a third of their lives, undergoing the process. Broadcasting is also an important agency for the transmission of culture; the average television viewer spends upwards of 15 hours a week with his set (see Belson 1967).

I have not dealt with science museums at all; I have mentioned only the prestige (and therefore cultural influence) of such organizations as the Royal Society, the Royal Institution, and the British Association. Again, although I gathered information on the subjects, I have not touched upon adult education (and its powerful new weapon the Open University), nor have I dealt with science publishing directed at laymen. And, no doubt, every reader will think of his own example.

I have tried to show that in education, at least up to university entrance level, there is wide scope for activity designed to offer science to non-specialists. Although some organizational problems are still crippling (in particular the shortage of science teachers and the lack, in many schools, of space and equipment) some remedies to the problem of scientific illiteracy are ready to hand. For example, I have tried to show (in Chapters 4 and 5) that the methods and content of public examinations are more open to modification by teachers than is often believed. The burden of fact, of which teachers and pupils alike complain, is not a necessary component of an examination; and it is within the power of teachers to influence the nature of the examinations set by the examining boards—who are quite literally 'in business', examining what schools choose to teach.

My views (in Chapter 6) about the possibilities of curriculum reform in universities may appear unduly pessimistic. In so far as preparation for university courses has become largely the *raison d'être* of G.C.E. A-level examinations, my pessimism should perhaps extend to the content and combination of A-level subjects taken by schoolchildren. But I have argued that the present tension could be greatly eased by modification of university entry requirements. In particular, there is evidence that many sixth-formers would, if the opportunity were there and prudence permitted, take a combination of arts and science subjects. Greater flexibility in university entry requirements could transform the educational scene.

Science is a social phenomenon. It is not therefore surprising to find that the principal objectives which one can propose for the science education of laymen are social ones. Nor, for that matter, is it surprising to find that the principal constraints are also social ones, concerned with the prestige of different types of examination irrespective of their educational excellences, or the professionalization and bureaucratization of science and technology. To have explored the consequences of the professionalization of science in depth would have required a book on the sociology of science. But I hope that my brief comments on the social context of science education will illuminate some of the reasons for the slowness of curriculum reform.

I would not want it to be thought that, because this book is primarily concerned with ways of removing constraints from the dissemination of science culture, that I believe science to be the characteristic or most desirable feature of our culture. Indeed, it must be emphasized that the most promising 'science' education of laymen does not separate science as something special. I have argued (in Chapter 3) that the 'integrated' approach of much primary school education is a model to be imitated at higher levels of the process of education. It is just as important, probably more important, that education transmits legal and moral cultural values than scientific ones. But if (as I argue in this book) there is value in providing science education for everyone, what ought to be done? Not everyone will be able, or would wish, to involve themselves with complex problems of science policy like those mentioned above. Nor would the avalanche of information into the National Lending Library be of any more concern to them than an avalanche in an uninhabited part of the Rockies. So why should science be of any interest to the layman? It is with this question that we must begin.

1 *Science for Non-Scientists*

WHY should science and technology be of any interest at all to non-scientists? For any discussion about ways of teaching science and technology to non-scientists to be meaningful, it is essential that this question should be answered. It is necessary to show first of all what science is, how it differs from technology, and how both science and technology are part of general culture. Then it is necessary to demonstrate how the individual, to develop his capabilities fully, should be able to enjoy as many aspects of the prevailing culture as possible.

At once one is faced with a difficulty: science is very difficult to define. Ziman (1968, p. 1) says that 'to answer the question "What is Science?" is almost as presumptuous as to try to state the meaning of life itself.' But at the risk of oversimplification, it is necessary to start with some description of science as an intellectual and social phenomenon, rather than just an accumulation of knowledge, to demonstrate its contribution to general culture. To avoid dogmatism, the following pages will rely as much as possible on the statements of practising scientists.

Bernal, for example (1954, p. 5) declined to define science:

science is so old, it has undergone so many changes in history, it is so linked at every point with other social activities, that any attempted definition, and there have been many, can only express more or less inadequately one of the aspects, often a minor one, that it has had at some period of its growth.

He went on to point out that science may variously be taken as an institution; as a method; as a cumulative tradition of knowledge; as a major factor in the maintenance and development of production; and as one of the most powerful influences moulding beliefs and attitudes to the universe and to man. He pointed out (op. cit., p. 7) that 'Science has already acquired so many of the characters of an exclusive profession, including that of long training and apprentice-ship, that it is popularly more easy to recognise a scientist than to know what science is. Indeed, an easy definition of science is *what scientists do.*'

1.1. Science as what scientists do

Scientists are people of very dissimilar temperaments doing different things in very different ways. Among scientists are collectors, classifiers and compulsive tidiers-up; many are detectives by temperament and many are explorers; some are artists and others artisans. There are poet-scientists and philosopher-scientists and even a few mystics. What sort of mind or temperament can all these people be supposed to have in common? (Medawar 1967, p. 132).

As Medawar points out there is clearly no such thing as a peculiarly scientific mind. Is there, then, a scientific method? The answer is almost certainly No. But perhaps the only way of discover-ing the peculiar qualities of science is by observing some of the particular methods which scientists use in their work. Some of these methods are mental; some are manual.

Apparatus and observations. Physical scientists are more easy to recognize than are social scientists because physical scientists often use apparatus. As Bernal (1954, p. 13) observed:

Scientific apparatus fulfils either of two major functions: as scientific instruments, such as telescopes or microscopes, it can be used to extend and make more precise our sensory perception of the world; as scientific tools, such as micro-manipulators, stills, or incubators, it can be used to extend, in a controlled way, our motor manipulation of the things around us.

In effect, what apparatus does is commonly to render observation independent of the particular observer—although it may have many other specific purposes. Indeed, one of the chief activities of the scientist is to observe in order to establish facts and relations be-tween facts that are as far as possible independent of his own senti-ments. This is in sharp contrast to the artist, who observes in order to transform what he sees into some new and evocative creation.

Although observation, generally with the aid of apparatus, is

frequently a characteristic of science, it is not in itself science. Medawar (1967, p. 114) has pointed out that the factual burden of a
science varies inversely with its degree of maturity.

As science advances, particular facts are comprehended within, and
therefore in a sense annihilated by, general statements of steadily increasing explanatory power and compass—whereupon the facts need no
longer be known explicitly, i.e., spelled out and kept in mind. In all
sciences we are being progressively relieved of the burden of singular
instances, the tyranny of the particular. We need no longer record the
fall of every apple.

How, then, does the process of observation become science?

Classification and measurement. Observations do not become
'facts' without some system of classification. Indeed, one can do
nothing with a new phenomenon until one has attempted to classify
it.Paske (1967, pp. 259–60) indicates some of the power of the activity
of classification by describing someone's reaction to learning that a
whale is not a fish but a mammal. This 'fact' cries out for explanation. How is it possible that an air-breathing animal which suckles
its young came to live in such an apparently hostile environment?
Paske points out that this and a thousand other questions can be
asked and answered only if the existence of whales is surprising, and
their existence is surprising only if they are categorized with animals
whose predominant domain is terrestrial.

Classificatory systems clearly raise questions. As Bernal (1954,
pp. 11–12) pointed out, measurement is just another stage of classification. Observations have to be put in order before anything can be
done with them. Measurement is only one further stage of that putting in order.

Counting is the ordering of one collection against another; in the last
resort against the fingers. Measuring is counting the number of a
standard collection that balance or line-up with the quantity that is to be
weighed or measured. It is measurement that links science with mathematics on the one hand, and with commercial and mechanical practice
on the other. It is by measurement that numbers and forms enter science,
and it is also by measurement that it is possible to indicate precisely what
has to be done to reproduce given conditions and obtain a desired result.

The first main point about science is now apparent. The collection
of data and its interpretation are programmatic rather than hap-

hazard. Scientists clearly know what they are looking for; they construct apparatus for very precise purposes.

Hypotheses. Experimentation is commonly believed to be the characteristic activity of scientists. Experiments are contrived experiences, which are undertaken to see if what was expected to happen does in fact happen; that is to say, they are undertaken to test out hypotheses.

Kuhn in *The structure of scientific revolutions* (1962) argues that paradigms (or collections of hypotheses) give the normal activities of scientists their characteristic shape. Mopping-up operations are what engage most scientists throughout their careers. A paradigm, Kuhn argues, forces scientists to examine some esoteric details in a depth that would otherwise be unimaginable. To take an example used by Medawar (1967) in a similar argument: rubbing two sticks together to see what happens is an experiment in Bacon's sense—a contrived experience which does not rely upon the luck of common observation. An experiment in the modern sense of the word would be to rub two sticks together to see if enough heat could be generated by friction to ignite them. The difference is that the modern experiment is based upon an hypothesis: that friction generates heat. A collection of such hypotheses forms a paradigm and paradigms provide the foci for most scientific investigations.

Kuhn (1962, pp. 25–33) shows how the construction of paradigms provides foci for factual scientific investigations. First, there are facts which a paradigm has shown to be important, or has made worth investigating in detail; for example, stellar positions and magnitudes in astronomy. Secondly, there are attempts to determine facts, without much intrinsic interest, which can be predicted by the theory. The existence of the paradigm sets the problem which the scientist tries to solve by whatever technique he can devise. Kuhn (1962, p. 26) cites special telescopes constructed to demonstrate the Copernican prediction of annual parallax; Atwood's machine devised to give the first unequivocal demonstration of Newton's second law; Foucault's apparatus to show that the speed of light is greater in air than in water. A third class of experiments and observation consists of empirical work undertaken to articulate the paradigm theory. Such work may be designed to resolve ambiguities or to solve problems to which the paradigm had drawn attention. For example, efforts to articulate a paradigm may aim at quantitative laws such as Boyle's law. As Kuhn (1962, p. 28) argues, a paradigm is necessary before the experiments become meaningful. A further kind of experiment may be used to articulate a paradigm, a type of experiment more like exploration. These experiments involve the application of the paradigm to ambiguous areas.

Kuhn goes on to argue that much of the theoretical manipulations of normal science are undertaken so that paradigms can be confronted directly with experiments. The experiments, in turn, are designed to display new applications of the paradigm or to increase the precision of an observation.

Science as puzzle-solving. Kuhn notes that it is a striking feature of normal research problems that they rarely aim to produce major novelties. Often every result of experimentation is known in advance. Kuhn maintains that to scientists the results gained in normal research are significant because they add to the scope and precision with which the paradigm can be applied. 'Bringing a normal research problem to a conclusion is achieving the anticipated in a new way, and it requires the solution of all sorts of complex instrumental, conceptual, and mathematical puzzles. The man who succeeds proves himself an expert puzzle-solver, and the challenge of the puzzle is an important part of what usually drives him on.' (Kuhn 1962, p. 36).

Paradigms, in Kuhn's argument, provide the strategy; puzzle-solving is the tactics. This is important, for, as Kuhn (1962, p. 37) argues '... one of the things a scientific community acquires with a paradigm is a criterion for choosing problems that, while the paradigm is taken for granted, can be assumed to have solutions. To a great extent these are the only problems that the community will admit as scientific or encourage its members to undertake.' Medawar was saying much the same thing when he observed that whereas politics is the art of the possible, science is the art of the soluble.

Science as a whole may have very grand objectives; scientists as people rarely do. As Kuhn (1962, p. 38) puts it:

The scientific enterprise as a whole does from time to time prove useful, open up new territory, display order, and test long-accepted belief. Nevertheless, *the individual* engaged on a normal research problem *is almost never doing any one of these things*. Once engaged, his motivation is of a rather different sort. What then challenges him is the conviction that, if only he is skilful enough, he will succeed in solving a puzzle that no-one before has solved or solved so well.

Kuhn's characterization of the normal activity of scientists as puzzle-solving is so illuminating that it is necessary to show why he uses the word 'puzzle'. He writes:

If it is to classify as a puzzle, a problem must be characterised by more than an assured solution. There must also be rules that limit both the nature of acceptable solutions and the steps by which they are to be obtained. To solve a jig-saw puzzle is not, for example, merely 'to make a picture'. Either a child or a contemporary artist could do that by scattering selected pieces, as abstract shapes, upon some neutral ground. The picture thus produced might be far better, and would certainly be more original, than the one from which the puzzle had been made. Nevertheless, such a picture would not be a solution. To achieve that all the pieces must be used, their plain sides must be turned down, and they must be interlocked without forcing until no holes remain. Those are among the rules that govern jig-saw puzzle solutions. Similar restrictions upon the admissible solutions of crossword puzzles, riddles, chess problems, and so on, are readily discovered.

The parallel with the activity of scientists is very compelling.

A paradigm provides, as it were, the rules of a game; the normal activity of science is the solving of the puzzle set by that game. Kuhn's main thesis is that when a paradigm throws up anomalies, normal science can do nothing about it. Normal science ultimately leads only to the recognition of anomalies and thence to crises. These crises of the scientific enterprise are terminated, not by deliberation and interpretation but by a relatively sudden and unstructured event like the gestalt switch. In this switch, the entire paradigm has to be supplanted by a new one (cf. pp. 121f.). That is to say, a new bundle of hypotheses has to be postulated so that the anomaly can be accommodated without violence to logic or experimental observation.

Medawar (1969, pp. 51–2) describes the paradigm-directed scientific activity as 'the hypothetico-deductive' scheme of thought. He lists various merits that this scheme has as good scientific methodology. For example, the scheme explains why a scientist chooses to make one set of observations rather than another. The hypothetico-deductive scheme provides a theory of special incentive. Observations no longer range over the universe of observables: they are confined to those that have a bearing on the hypothesis under investigation. Again, the scheme allows for the continual rectification or running adjustment of hypotheses by a process of negative feedback. Or again, the hypothetico-deductive scheme gives due weight to the critical purposes of experimentation: experiments are more often carried out to discriminate between possibilities than to enlarge the stockpile of factual information.

Ziman (1968) has stressed the importance of consensus in the process. Science, he argues (pp. 9–11), is not merely *published* knowledge or information. Anyone can make an observation, or conceive a hypothesis; scientific knowledge is more than this. The objective of science is not just to acquire information or to utter all non-contradictory notions; its goal is a consensus of rational opinion over the widest possible field. Every scientist Ziman argues, sees through his own eyes—and also through the eyes of his predecessors and colleagues. It is never one individual who goes through all the steps in the process; it is a group of individuals, dividing their labour but continuously and jealously checking each others' contributions. The cliché of scientific prose betrays itself: 'Hence *we* arrive at the conclusion that ...' The audience to which scientific publications are addressed is not passive; by its cheering or booing, its bouquets or brickbats, it actively controls the substance of the communications that it receives. In Ziman's view, it is meaningless to try to distinguish between science as a body of knowledge, science as what scientists do, and science as a social institution.

Science and social purpose. From the foregoing discussion, it should be apparent that science is primarily concerned with how. As Bernal (1954, p. 16) said: 'Its mode is indicative—it shows people how to do what they want to do.' Where the wish comes from is another matter:

'Every work of science has a purpose and generates a further purpose, but that purpose is not the characteristically scientific aspect of the work, neither is it the beauty nor pleasure to be appreciated in the work of science. In its purely scientific aspect, it is a recipe: it tells you how to carry out certain things if you want to do them.'

Clearly, it is possible for the paradigm-oriented, puzzle-solving activity of science to be motivated by sheer curiosity about the physical environment. It is equally possible for it to be motivated by a variety of other purposes: for example, a metaphysical desire to detect order in the universe; a moral desire to relieve suffering through understanding of disease; the desire for approbation or power; or even simply the desire to earn a living in safety and security. The important point is that the actual activity of science is morally neutral; the moment science is put to social, economic, political, or other use, it not only ceases to be science, it also takes on social significance. As Bridgham (1969, pp. 36–7) has observed, it is probably too easy to say that science seeks explanation of the environment while technology seeks its control and exploitation. The two now seem too closely related and interdependent to be distinguished by any simple definition. However, he notes:

> Over the past 200–300 years, our science and our technology have moved closer together; in many cases, terminology and specific procedures are shared by workers in allied areas of science and technology, and it is not too difficult for a single individual to shuttle back and forth between scientific and technological problems. Still, the two are not the same. The criteria for the appraisal of scientific work and of technological work may be different and so may be the procedures for appraisal. If science is characterised by a community sharing a paradigm, then that community must eventually be convinced of the value of a piece of scientific work, or the work has no scientific value. The technologist, on the other hand, may appeal the judgment of his peers to the larger community of potential users of technology. The value of a piece of technological work is ultimately determined by its market; the value of a piece of scientific work is determined by the scientists' peers.

It is clear that puzzle-solving science can be an element of general culture in more than one way.

1.2. Science, technology, and general culture

It is precisely because the puzzle-solving approach of science has been applied in recent years to technology that technology and science have become confused with each other. It is principally through technology that science impinges upon general culture.

Culture has been defined by sociologists as the reaction to and handling of environment by groups of people. For discussion, it is convenient to identify two aspects of culture: instrumental culture is concerned with the way in which a social group controls its environment, social and physical. Instrumental aspects of culture are therefore recognized and described in terms of their social, political, economic, moral, and other purposes. Expressive culture is concerned with the reaction to environment of groups of people. Music, poetry, philosophy, and history, for example, as expressive aspects of culture, reflect a community's belief about its environment. Academically, expressive culture is recognized and described through the concepts by which individuals classify, describe, and react to their environment. It has been noted above that the maturity of science (as an aspect of expressive culture) is inversely proportional to its factual burden. That is to say, the methods by which physical scientists handle facts lead to increasingly sophisticated hypotheses; and the expressive value of a science is measured in terms of economy of hypothesis. Although it is helpful to distinguish between instrumental and expressive culture in trying to describe the purpose of any item in a culture, the distinction can be misleading. Clearly, expressive aspects of culture may determine the purpose or objectives of instrumental aspects of culture. Conversely, the instrumental aspects of culture inevitably express something of the beliefs of the community.

Technology may be described as the systematic and purposeful extension of human faculties. For example, the telephone is the extension of speech and hearing; a spade or mechanical digger is an extension of the hand; clothes are the extension of our skin; and so on. It is, indeed, difficult to name a technological device or system which is not an extension of one or other of our human faculties.

The connections between science, technology, and general culture become apparent when one considers the uses to which we put our faculties. Basically, we use our faculties either to transmit information or to manipulate material. To put it another way, we use our faculties either to express our ideas and beliefs or to manipulate material to meet needs which are in turn expressions of our beliefs. The speed, ease, and efficiency with which we can manipulate material is closely related to the efficiency with which we can describe our purpose in manipulating it and can identify the most suitable methods for doing so. This is where the puzzle-solving tactics of science, when applied to technology, have produced astonishing results.

Wealth is created by the manipulation of materials to meet specific demand. Demand is discovered and described by processes of information handling. It is not difficult to see that when the hypothetico-deductive scheme of thought is applied to technology, the effect is cumulative. Material is manipulated more effectively; demand is discovered and described more clearly; and material can then be manipulated to meet demand.

It is here that the impact of technology, and therefore of science, on the community is most clearly seen. The distribution of wealth is an economic problem. In so far as the 'laws' of economics are understood, it becomes possible in theory to manipulate material and handle information efficiently to meet defined human needs. But any shift in the distribution of wealth must involve a conflict of human wishes. Even if the application of science to a technological problem results in the creation of wealth for one sector of the community, it is inevitable that another sector of the community will become, if not poorer, at least comparatively less well off. Politics is concerned with the achievement of equilibrium—locally, nationally, internationally—in the potentially unstable situation brought about by differing ideas concerning the distribution of wealth. For any political action to be possible, it is necessary for politicians (and, consequently, those who vote them into office or condone their staying in office) to formulate clear programmes for the distribution of wealth. It is clearly impossible for any politician or any small or large group of politicians to possess all the information which would render their system for distributing wealth 'absolutely' just. Politicians must choose the programmes of action which they think 'best' for their fellow-men. 'Best' may be described in a variety of ways: in terms of freedom from governmental control of activity; freedom from ill-health; freedom from oppression by internal or external violence; and so on. Ultimately decisions about what to do with wealth are based upon the ideologies of politicians and of their supporters.

In so far as technology contributes to the possibilities of distributing wealth (by the manipulation of material or by the handling of information) it is the fundamental part of the whole complex process. That is to say, any artefact or system devised by a technologist will have the potential to affect the economic system. It therefore raises political questions which in turn involve moral or ideological ones.

Every culture has technology. Indeed, one can even describe different cultures in terms of their technologies: we speak of the Iron Age, the Stone Age, the Bronze Age. When one visits another country, it is the technological aspects which first strike one: the techniques of house-building, the techniques of cooking and storing food, etc. These are reactions to environment (and especially climate); they also express in a fundamental way the beliefs of the community. A visitor might, for example see people eating yoghourt out of cartons. At first sight, yoghourt-eating might appear a less dramatic manifestation of culture than cathedrals or paintings. However, the fact that yoghourt is eaten at all is an indication of a belief that it is not poisonous, but nourishing. Then, the carton is itself significant. Theoretically, one could have yoghourt dispensed directly into one's hand in the market-place, but this would be highly inconvenient. Yoghourt cartons can thus be seen as aspects of instrumental culture. The particular sizes and shapes of the cartons are expressions of economic forces of the market-place. By and large, it is not possible to buy yoghourt in any quantity one wishes; one is constrained to buy certain defined quantities. To produce non-uniform containers for yoghourt to meet the wishes of individuals would be more expensive. Manufacturers have presumably taken steps to discover the quantity of yoghourt the average person requires at any one time, and, more important, the amount he is prepared to pay. Again, the fact that we expect to throw away the empty carton is a further aspect of our culture. In order, presumably, to save time and effort, we are prepared to pay more money for disposable cartons rather than, say, bottles which could be used repeatedly in the same way as milk bottles. As individual citizens we may have very little say in the matter of how we would like to buy yoghourt. The fact that we acquiesce in the chosen method is, however, expressive (an expressive item of culture) of our system of values. These values are disguised by the fact that we can translate one into another by means of money, for money is stored time, stored effort, stored value, a uniform method of measuring different social values. The money we pay for cartons of yoghourt represents, in a very real way, part of ourselves—the part of ourselves poured out in our work for which we receive remuneration.

The choice of yoghourt as an example is not purely frivolous. In preparing yoghourt for human consumption and for mass distribution, technologists must have solved many puzzles in the fields of biochemistry and of mechanics. The puzzles would have involved decisions about the mixture of substances which constitutes the yoghourt we buy and the type of material suitable for containers. In the interests of profitability, it is highly likely that the manufacturers systematically attacked problems of how to mix substances to give the most pleasing taste, and how to make a sufficiently durable container for the least possible cost. Although the end-product was clearly technological, it is highly likely that many principles of science were brought to bear upon the problem. Indeed, it is even possible that in tackling this particular problem new principles were discovered.

It would not be difficult to choose more dramatic examples of the symbiosis of science and technology in modern society. The articulation of scientific paradigms requires measuring instruments and other tools of ever-increasing complexity; the propagation of technology, in turn, requires ever more accurate and detailed descriptions of natural phenomena. It would not be difficult to demonstrate the extent to which the ordinary citizen uses, in his daily life, hundreds of products of sophisticated technology, and, in like manner, to demonstrate that the technology behind these products is based upon the solution of scientific problems and may in turn have thrown up new problems which scientists have tackled. However, it is quite possible to go through life using the most advanced products of technology without ever considering the science upon which they are based. What real relevance does science culture have for the layman?

1.3. The non-scientist in a science culture

If tomorrow all search for material knowledge for its own sake were to cease, the change would go unnoticed for generations, perhaps forever. We already have so great a store of facts and techniques that their gainful exploitation could go on without any new principle being discovered. A stable civilisation could come into being, settled on a higher technological level than any civilisation of the past but as technically unprogressive as any of them. The man who made his dugout canoe worked to rule-of-thumb, repeating what someone else had shown him. So does nearly every man helping to build an aeroplane. We could go on making the same kind of aeroplanes, television sets, textiles, drugs, without any change in design, quite long enough for new generations to grow up quite unacquainted with 'natural philosophy'.

In his paper 'Notes towards the definition of a scientific culture', Greenaway (1958) speculated whether science can become a part of the common tradition of the educated man in the same way as art, literature, religion, and political institutions. He noted, as has been described above, that science is already part of our tradition: that the world is science-ridden, and can never again be independent of it. Much of our technology is based upon scientific discovery. However, innovative science is practised by a highly-educated élite, and it is doubtful whether the layman can ever have direct experience of it. Indeed, Greenaway suggested that one of the reasons why the layman cannot be exposed directly to innovative science is the practice of publication of scientific papers. He noted (op. cit., p. 29) that even fairly mediocre pieces of work can be published in scientific journals of a very narrow specialist scope.

The process of assessment by impartial referees still selects before publication, the mediocre which gets through subsides into obscurity, the original and fertile eventually produces its effect after scientific approval and verification. Nevertheless, the bulk of this written self-expression never finds its way into the common stream of literature because it is never assessed by any other merits than the stimulus it may give to further experiment, or the gainful utility of its information. The operation of the criteria of scientific excellence has two effects on the paper considered as a literary product. It drains out of the effort of composition any literary content or beauty of language, metaphor, hyperbole and so forth which might hinder the operation of the machinery of scientific assessment, so that the non-scientific reader finds nothing there to read even if the material is intrinsically intelligible. Secondly, the young scientist is given nothing to emulate but those qualities in the paper which will guarantee scientific survival.

In short, it is the professionalization and bureaucratization of modern science that has rendered it relatively inaccessible to the layman. Granted that the layman can enjoy many of the technological fruits of scientific speculation, are there any major reasons why the non-scientist should understand explicitly what is implicit in the science culture he enjoys?

In the next chapter, some possible objectives of science education for non-specialists will be considered. In subsequent chapters methods of approach in achieving these objectives, in testing them, and in organizing educational activity will be discussed. Meanwhile, two important aspects of science culture which affect the layman bear mention.

First, one of the principal functions of expressive culture is to indicate to the individual who he is. In any community, an individual learns who he is by comparing himself with other people and with other things. He can learn of the exploits of heroes of his society from popular songs and ballads; he can learn correct behaviour by contemplating deviates as portrayed in drama; he can see the relationship of himself to the physical world in paintings; he learns his moral duties not only from newspapers but from religious activity, and he measures himself against other individuals and against the forces of nature by participating in sports. King Lear when asking 'Who is it can tell me who I am?' received the answer 'Lear's fool'. Today, he might be answered 'Lear's scientist'. The scientist has produced an abundance of descriptions of man to complement and contrast with previous descriptions. To this extent, the 'cultivated' individual can learn of his identity in his culture through a whole new range of dimensions not previously available. Just as he can learn what it means to be a Briton by reading the history of the British people, so he can learn what it is to be *Homo sapiens* by reading of Man's similarities to and differences from other mammals. He can learn what is the biochemical basis of his nature. That is to say, science provides a whole new range of modes of expressive culture by which the individual can find his identity.

Secondly, science is an important part of instrumental culture, not only by virtue of its association with technology but also because it is a formidable type of question-asking. That is to say, science can demonstrate the possibility of choice where previously no choice was believed to exist. Built into any scientific investigation is a programme of intention. As noted above, scientific experiments are not undertaken haphazardly; they are constructed to test hypotheses. It is not necessary for the layman to know in detail how a particular hypothesis may be tested, nor is it necessary for him to know in detail the results of the testing, but his life can be greatly enriched if he knows the reason why particular questions are being asked, and what sorts of answers may be expected.

It could be argued that these two reasons for non-scientists participating actively in science culture are, as it were, options. It could equally well be argued that they are now political necessities. Large sums of the taxpayers' money are spent each year in the pursuit of science—not simply of technology. It is surely highly desirable that as many members of the lay public as possible be able to at least ask the fundamental question: Why are you doing this? of any scientist engaged in an expensive activity. Again, the activities of scientists are throwing up many questions to which science itself cannot produce answers. For example, research into the transplantation of organs from one human being to another has posed acute moral problems (the more sophisticated the method of measuring bodily functions, the more difficult it is to identify the precise moment of death). It is of the utmost importance that the issues be as clearly defined as possible. It might be argued that the burden should lie on the scientists who are carrying out the experiments. It can equally well be argued that there is an increasing need for the ordinary non-scientist citizen to know what sort of questions science can answer and what sort of questions fall in the province of the lawyer and the philosopher.

Whether they like it or not, non-scientists are today involved in a science culture which involves the expenditure of vast sums of public money; which produces moral dilemmas; which offers staggering possibilities of imaginative exploration. The principal method by which culture is transmitted in western society is through education; it is, therefore, to the objectives of science education for non-scientists that we now turn.

2 Objectives and Methods of Science Education for Non-Scientists

To disentangle, as far as possible, intrinsic academic constraints from the social ones with which later chapters will be concerned, it will be useful to review the main general objectives of science education for non-scientists. Clearly, the appropriateness of different objectives will depend very much upon the abilities of individual pupils and students, and also upon their interests. Even those who will become professional scientists are to some extent at a disadvantage in sciences other than those in which they are specialists. It will, therefore, be useful to highlight the particular values embodied in science education—which should be the same for science specialists as for non-scientists.

Whatever methods of teaching are adopted to achieve the main general objectives of science education, social constraints will make themselves felt. However, there are intrinsic academic advantages and disadvantages in the different methods which can be used. Before going into the details of methods actually used, it is therefore useful to examine what might be called 'ideal types' of method to see what these factors are.

Finally, it is necessary to comment briefly on some of the major effects of examinations which, in theory, should indicate whether the methods of teaching used are meeting the objectives prescribed.

This chapter is, then, a theoretical prelude to subsequent chapters which will deal primarily with practice.

2.1. Some objectives of science education for non-scientists
(a) *Science and practical problems*

In two articles, Weaver (1957, 1966) has emphasized the extent to which our daily lives are surrounded by problems with scientific implications. Former generations have had similar problems, and have resorted to 'authorities', old-wives'-tales, proverbs, and so on to find solutions. Nowadays we not only have the problems themselves but also the problem of wondering whether or not there is a solution to a particular problem.

The problem for the modern citizen is knowing when in a particular case there is an 'answer' to his particular problem, or whether he must exercise personal judgement. For example, Weaver lists the following questions: when do we—or do we not—consult the psychiatrist or accept a free dose of a new serum? What sort of vitamins do we need and where can we get them? What are hormones and what are the known effects of tampering with the balance of them in ourselves? How do sleeping pills and tranquillizers work? What nutritional régimes and slimming schedules, if any, are worth adopting and under what circumstances? How do we know whether our children have emotional and psychological problems or if they are not simply behaving the way children always do? How can one tell whether the birth-rate, death-rate, and population increase is a problem or not? On what basis can food supplies be calculated? How do we know whether or not cigarette smoking causes lung cancer? What sort of factors affect fertility and what are the causes of birth defects?

To list these questions is not to suggest than any individual non-scientist citizen can possibly know all the answers. It may, however, be sensible to provide him with enough education to know what sort of questions should be asked and to whom he should go for answers. When he has found somebody prepared to give the answers, he ought perhaps to know how to judge the results.

(b) *De-mystifying science*

The activities of scientists profoundly affect our daily lives. If science is to continue to receive an adequate supply of public funds, it is important that the public have a favourable image of scientists—an image which does not err on the side of superstitious awe, nor on the side of fear and mistrust. Ritchie Calder (1964) has commented that science, which exists to remove mystery and magic, has created its own mystery and its own magic. Dupree (1961) even identified what he called the cargo cult approach to science. He notes (op. cit., p. 717) how in the Second World War the natives of Melanesia saw the terrible and wonderful end-products of western

C

technology coming ashore as cargo from fleets of ships. They could see neither the industrial system nor the pattern of ideas which produced these unimagined riches. Their reaction, however, was based both on close observation and on cause-and-effect reasoning. The white men who possessed the cargo engaged in mysterious paper-passing rituals and erected monuments to their gods, with whom those who possessed the secret of the cargo could communicate, thus bringing more ships and more cargo. By grafting these observations of bureaucracy and radio technology on to stories of a Messiah, as half-understood from missionaries, and on to assorted native myths, the islanders were soon seized with the millenial ecstasy of the cargo cult. They stopped work, neglected their tribal customs and built bamboo antennas on their huts in order to communicate with the new Messiah who would bring the cargo to them. Dupree suggests that, without pressing the analogy too far, one can identify cargo cults in modern western society. Scientists appear as white-coated witch-doctors manipulating the mysteries of an esoteric cult. The public, failing to understand science, nevertheless worships it as a Messiah while fearing its diabolical power. Technological marvels, called science by the cults, add to their undeniable power by corroding the fabric of society with the false hope of an immediate millennium.

In similar vein, Holton (1960), discussing modern science and the intellectual tradition, identified other attitudes to science which are by no means healthy. For example, he notes the long-standing image of the scientist as iconoclast. Many scientific advances have been interpreted, either triumphantly or with apprehension, as blows against religion. To some extent, this situation is more the fault of theologians than of scientists; the theological position of the 'god of the gaps' has probably done more damage to theology than anything else. However, science and atheism are still closely linked in many people's minds. Again, Holton has noted an image of science as that of a force which can invade, possess, pervert, and destroy man. This image is of the psychopathic investigator of science fiction or the nuclear destroyer—immoral if he develops the weapons he is asked to produce, traitorous if he refuses. According to this view, scientific morality is inherently negative. It blights culture and leads to regimentation and to the impoverishment of life. Science is seen as the serpent seducing us into eating the fruits of the tree of knowledge and thereby dooming us. Holton bemoans the

fact that while it is not fashionable to confess to a lack of knowledge of the latest ephemera in literature or the arts, one may even
exhibit a touch of pride in professing ignorance of the structure of
the universe or one's own body or of the behaviour of matter or
one's own mind.

Mead and Métraux (1957) found that while the image of science
among high-school students was good, the image of scientists was
not. It has been said that every civilization lives only fifteen years
away from barbarism. That is to say, civilization has only fifteen
years in which to tame the newborn savage and turn him into a
responsible citizen. So, although the evidence from the Mead-
Métraux survey is now some years out of date, it provides a salutary
warning of the sorry image which scientists may get if science is
not adequately taught in schools. Science, Mead and Métraux report (1957, pp. 386f.), is a very broad field which may be seen as a
single unit, as a mélange, or as composed of entities (biology and
physics and chemistry) linked together by the personality of the
scientist. Science was seen by the 35 000 students participating in the
study as natural science with little direct reference to man as a
social being except in so far as the products of science—medicine
and bombs—affect his life. More important than the corporate
image of science is the shared image of the scientist. He is seen as a
man who wears a white coat and works in a laboratory. He is
elderly or middle-aged and wears glasses. He is surrounded by
equipment: a jungle gym of blown glass tubes and weird machines
with dials. He writes neatly in black notebooks.

At this point, Mead and Métraux note, the image of the scientist
diverges. On the positive side he is seen as a very intelligent man, a
genius or almost a genius. He has long years of expensive training
during which he studies very hard. He is interested in his work and
takes it seriously; he is careful, patient, devoted, courageous, open-
minded. He knows his subject. He works for long hours in the
laboratory, sometimes day and night, going without food and sleep.
He is prepared to work for years without getting results and faces
the possibility of failure without discouragement; he will try again.
He wants to know the answer. One day he may straighten up and
shout: 'I've found it. I've found it.' He is a dedicated man who
works not for money or fame or self-glory but for the benefit of
mankind and the welfare of his country. However, there is a negative side of this image of the scientist. The scientist is a brain. He

spends his days indoors, sitting in a laboratory, pouring things from one test-tube into another. His work is uninteresting, dull, monotonous, tedious, time-consuming, and though he works for years, he may see no results or may fail and he is likely to receive neither adequate recompense nor recognition. He may live in a cold-water flat; his laboratory may be dingy. His work may be dangerous: chemicals may explode, he may be hurt by radiation, or he may die. If he does medical research, he may bring home disease, or may use himself as a guinea-pig, or may even accidentally kill somebody. He may not believe in God or may lose his religion. His belief that man is descended from animals is disgusting. He is so involved in his work that he doesn't know what is going on in the world. He has no other interests and neglects his body for his mind. He can only talk, eat, breathe, and sleep science. He neglects his family, pays no attention to his wife, never plays with his children. He has no social life, no other intellectual interests, no hobbies or relaxations. He bores his wife, his children and their friends (for he has no friends of his own or knows only other scientists) with incessant talk that no one can understand; or else he pays no attention or has secrets he cannot share. He is always reading a book. He brings home work and also bugs and creepy things. A scientist should not marry. No one wants to be such a scientist or to marry him (op. cit., p. 387).

Mead and Métraux note that this image is one which is likely to invoke a negative attitude as far as personal career or marriage choice is concerned. The number of ways in which the image of the scientist contains extremes which appear to be contradictory—too much contact with money or too little; being bald or bearded; confined work indoors, or travelling far away; talking all the time in a boring way, or never talking at all—all these represent deviations from the accepted way of life, from being a normal friendly human being, who lives like other people and gets along with other people (op. cit., p. 388).

The effects of such an image, not only on the marriage prospects of scientists but also on the public credibility of science as an activity, are of serious importance. Clearly, the image of scientists is likely to vary from year to year for a variety of cultural reasons. However, granted that modern western society has become extremely complex and depends for its survival upon the activities of scientists and of technologists, it is not unreasonable that one of the chief objectives of science education for the non-scientist should simply be to maintain a reasonably accurate (and if possible reasonably favourable) image of the scientist.

(c) *The ethics of observation*

Would it be too much to say that in the natural sciences today the given social environment has made it very easy for even an emotionally unstable person to be exact and impartial in his laboratory? The traditions he inherits, his instruments, the high degree of specialization, the crowd of witnesses that surround him, so to speak (if he publishes his results)—these all exert pressures that make impartiality on matters of *his* science almost automatic. Let him deviate from the rigorous role of impartial experimenter or observer at his peril; he knows all too well what a fool so and so made of himself by blindly sticking to a set of observations or a theory now clearly recognized to be in error. (Conant, 1946, p. 19.)

While emphasizing the tradition of impartiality required of the scientist in his laboratory, Conant concluded that as human beings scientific investigators are statistically distributed over the whole spectrum of human folly and wisdom much as other men. However, a third main objective for the teaching of science to non-specialists is that the ethics of observation, or the tradition of impartiality, as a characteristic of the scientific endeavour, should be brought to bear upon as many situations as possible.

Hoagland in *Science and the new humanism* (1960) suggests that science, like all other systems of thought, seeks answers to questions which men hold to be of importance. But, whereas in other disciplines answers are accepted that harmonize with particular world-views and mythologies peculiar to different special cultural groups, science seeks answers which are reducible to everyone's experience. The fact that, by virtue of its specialized jargon, science may not be successful in this respect is beside the point. Hoagland's main point is that truth as developed by scientific activity can become a source of social values. It can however do so, he argues (op. cit., p. 112), only when a whole society, or a large part of it, accepts the assumption that no belief will survive, regardless of its attraction in terms of wishful thinking, if it conflicts with factual truth. This means setting-up the discovery of truth as an important social end, not only for the individual but for society as a whole. No society, he comments, has ever been really dedicated to this end. But there are varying degrees of such concern. In a scientifically oriented society the quest for truth is the important thing, even though we know that ultimate, final truth is not to be found.

In discussing 'the place of science in a liberal education' Ernest Nagel (1959) emphasized the role of science as the code of a community. Although the techniques of different sciences may differ, Nagel argued that what is distinctive of all science, not merely of natural science such as physics, and what assures the general reliability of scientific findings, is the use of a *common intellectual method* for assessing the weight of the available evidence for a proposed solution of a problem, and for accepting or rejecting a tentative conclusion of an inquiry. Scientific method, he suggested, is a procedure of applying logical canons for *testing* claims to knowledge (op. cit., p. 59). The history of science, he argued, makes it amply clear that the method of science is a more permanent part of the scientific enterprise than are most of the substantive conclusions asserted at any given time. The conclusions are generally corrected or replaced by more adequate ones with the progress of inquiry; but the intellectual method, though frequently refined, and extended, has proved itself so repeatedly successful in producing reliable knowledge that substantial changes in it are neither required nor likely.

Nagel (1959, p. 62) argued that the institution of science provides a mechanism for discovering the truth irrespective of personal idiosyncrasies, but without curtailing the rights of its members to develop freely their own insights and to dissent from accepted beliefs. The success of the scientific enterprise depends upon a sort of ethics of observation. It is for this reason that Nagel and others argue that science with its built-in ideals has a rightful place in general education in society.

(d) *Science and order*

A fourth major objective in the teaching of science to non-specialists is concerned with displaying the organizing principles of science. Because this objective is so closely related to the methods by which science is taught to non-specialists, it will be discussed at greater length below. However, it can be argued that one of the great attractions of physical science is that the organizing principles by which we may understand the interrelationships of phenomena are readily demonstrable. The phenomena themselves may, of course, be of intense interest. However, as has been argued in Chapter 1, it is theory that turns observation into fact, and paradigm that turns theory into intellectual construct. A major objective of science education for non-specialists is, therefore, to show the power of ordering concepts—even if they turn out to be wrong. As Nowell-Smith (1958) has argued, not every student can hope to become a Galileo, but to be a scientist is not to know what Galileo knew and more, it is to be able to understand, within the limits of one's capacity, how men like Galileo think. 'To know that momentum is the product of mass and velocity and to know that it is conserved is no doubt useful. But it is not in the completed theories and formulae that the educative value of science lies; it is in insight which it can give into the process of theory construction' (op. cit., p. 6). Ernest Nagel too argues (1959) that the student of science should be made aware that the introduction of quantitative distinctions is not a denial of qualitative differences but on the contrary is a means for identifying such differences in a more discriminating manner than is customary in everyday affairs. He also suggests that the chief objective of methodological emphasis is to make explicit that science is not mechanical routine, and that even on the most elementary levels of achievement, it involves the use of a disciplined but sophisticated imagination.

One of the major objectives of science education for non-specialists should, therefore, be to show the imaginative quality of the scientific enterprise.

(e) *Familiarity with major phenomena and ideas*

Not only do the major organizing principles of science have imaginative value to the non-scientist but so also do some of the major phenomena and ideas discovered by scientific enterprise. The difficulty of deciding precisely which major ideas and phenomena should be taught will be discussed below. However, apart from the usefulness of some knowledge of certain scientific ideas and principles in solving practical problems (see Section (a) above), there are the obvious benefits to non-scientists in knowing some principles for use in science-based hobbies such as photography, gardening, natural history or astronomy. But the major justification is neither for the immediate usefulness of the ideas, nor for their hobby value. It is because the discovery of ideas is as important as, if not more important than, the discovery of continents in previous years.

It should be clear from what has been said about these general objectives of science education for non-specialists that the kind of understanding of science which is being described necessarily involves experience of science. Knowing about science is not enough. The overall objective is one of subjective identification. Just as one of the traditional aims in teaching the humanities is to give a student the feeling of, say, what it would have been like to have lived in seventeeth-century England, what it would be like to live in Zambia, what it feels like to view the world through the mind of a major poet, so in teaching science to non-scientists it must be a major aim to let the non-scientist feel what it would be like to be a scientist. This is where difficulty begins. With the five main objectives in mind, it is now necessary to specify in more detail specific objectives which might govern the science education of non-specialists.

Some specific objectives of science for non-specialists

A scientist is recognized not only by what he knows and what he does but also by what he feels about what he knows and what he does. Ideally, a scientist has a consistent philosophy of life; a scientific conscience which is brought to bear upon all the problems which life may present. In practice, not unnaturally, scientists often exhibit these ideal qualities only in the laboratory, and outside the laboratory are very much the same as other men. It is, however, a worth-while objective of science education for non-specialists to provide the student with the in-the-laboratory experience of science and to hope that the attitudes associated with this experience will carry over to a certain extent into daily life.

Most classifications of educational objectives distinguish between knowledge and skills, and modes of thought and attitudes. For example, the *Report on the teaching of general science* (1950) of the Science Masters' Association (now the Association for Science Education) suggested (pp. 119–21) that the teaching and examining of general science should be concerned with: (1) acquisition of scientific information and knowledge—knowledge of empirical facts; power of reproducing, verbally, laws or principles; knowledge of technical terms, or of words used in science; ability to identify forms, structures, processes and to state their functions; power of explaining verbally the meaning of a law or a principle; (2) development of scientific modes of thought—ability to use scientific knowledge to explain facts of ordinary life, unification of experiences;

enlargement of experience by recognizing in ordinary life instances of the operation of natural laws; capacity to distinguish between facts and hypotheses; isolation of relevant facts from a complex situation; ability to plan experiments and to test statements; ability to apply generalizations to new problems; ability to draw reasonable generalizations from experimental data; ability to recognize problems which lend themselves to scientific treatment, and the contrary; (3) application of scientific knowledge to socially desirable ends, such as the ability to recognize situations or unsolved problems in which scientific knowledge could usefully be employed; (4) practical powers or skills, such as the development of manual skill and dexterity; the ability to handle scientific material and apparatus (i.e., skill in laboratory technique); development of ideals of careful, neat and accurate work; ability to apply scientific knowledge to solve the practical problems of everyday life; ability to devise experiments and to carry them through.

In similar manner, the Science Panel of the North-West Regional Curriculum Development Project (Rudd 1968) distinguished between skills and attitudes in their list of objectives. For example, among the skills they thought desirable for the 16-year-old school-leaver were: abilty to reproduce simple diagrammatic representations of uncomplicated systems; ability to read measuring equipment to a sensible order of accuracy and to understand the significance of a reading or set of readings; ability to make a record of readings or observations, and to know which of these are, and are not, relevant; ability to use simple graphical techniques; ability to relate the experimental results to a specific problem in a different, generally more explicitly related case; ability to communicate any 'discovery' or finding to their peers or superiors (op. cit., p. 3). Among the attitudes the Science Panel hoped to inculcate were, for example, care for the use of words, for equipment and apparatus; awareness of order, pattern and function in a man-made world, together with natural order and pattern-growing crystals, large molecules; appreciation of good workmanship; confidence, for example in the work of a group or in the success of a methodological approach as opposed to emotive (non-thinking) responses to a problem, irrespective of the setting of that problem (op. cit., p. 4).

Perhaps the most thorough and detailed explanation of how general objectives can be translated into specific ones is the *Taxonomy of educational objectives* (Bloom *et al.* 1956, Krathwohl, Bloom, and Masia 1956). In the cognitive domain, Bloom and his colleagues put forward a hierarchy of testable educational objectives of increasing abstraction. These range from knowledge (of specifics, of terminology, of conventions, of classification and categories, of methodology, etc.) through comprehension (which subsumes translation, interpretation, and extrapolation) to application, analysis, and synthesis of, for example, a unique communication or a set of abstract relations, and culminating in evaluation, the making of judgements about the value for some purpose of ideas, works, solutions, methods, or material.

Evaluation of an activity overlaps to a certain extent with the affective objectives which are treated in detail in the taxonomy of Krathwohl and his colleagues. The Krathwohl taxonomy seeks to grade the levels of interest shown by a student in a subject into a hierarchy similar to that used in the cognitive domain. For example, at the lowest level of the hierarchy is simple receiving (attending to a subject). As a student becomes more interested in a subject or an activity, he exhibits a range of behaviours from simple responding to ultimately characterization by a value or value-complex. In science, at this highest stage of the taxonomy of affective objectives, the individual is likely to have become a scientist. Scientific values are likely to be not only organized into some kind of internally consistent system but also to control the behaviour of the individual. For example, a person who has become a 'scientist' in this meaning of the word is likely to be ready to revise judgements and to change his behaviour in the light of evidence. He is likely to be willing to face facts and the conclusions which can be logically drawn from them; to view problems in objective, realistic, and tolerant terms; and to rely increasingly upon the methods of science for finding answers to questions about the physical world and also about society.

It should be clear that for a student to use the ethics of observation in his daily life, he would in fact need to be characterized by a whole set of values normally only found in a scientist—and then only in the scientist's professional work. That is to say, in terms of Krathwohl's taxonomy of affective objectives, the non-scientist student might be expected to reach the highest level of abstraction. Clearly, it is difficult to devise a satisfactory education for a non-scientist which meets such objectives. But the problem is not insuperable. Achieving such objectives depends not so much upon the quantity of scientific education as upon its quality; and the quality of education depends very much upon the methods used.

2.2. Some methods by which science may be taught to non-scientists

There are many ways in which non-scientists can be exposed to science. Setting aside for the moment the prodigious difficulties of time-tabling, staffing, examining, and so on, it is useful to examine some of these methods in the light of the general and specific objectives listed in the previous section. This list of methods is not intended to be definitive, nor is it assumed that any one of the methods will be used in isolation—although all those discussed have in fact been used in the past. It is possible that some creative combination of methods will best suit the needs of any group of non-scientists at a particular level of education.

Yudkin (1969) studied the ways in which American colleges sought to teach science to arts undergraduates. He lists (pp. 114–15) three typical attempts to justify undergraduate courses given in different American colleges, as follows:

Course A. The broad objectives of the course are:
1. To provide an understanding of those phases of science which affect the individual as a person, and in family and community relationships;
2. To provide an understanding of the place of science in society;
3. To provide an understanding of the scientific attitude and method, in so far as they can serve as tools in dealing with everyday problems of living;
4. To furnish a foundation for the building of an adequate world view.

Course B. The purposes of the course are:
1. To lead to an adequate understanding on the part of the student of the major facts and principles of the physical sciences;
2. To develop the ability of the student to do critical thinking in the physical sciences;
3. To develop certain desirable changes in attitude on the part of the individual student;
4. To develop in the student a sensitiveness to the social values and implications of the sciences.

Course C. The aims of the course are to gain:
1. Familiarity with certain present-day concepts in physical sciences;
2. An appreciation of scientific methods as a way of dealing with problems;
3. An understanding of the impact of scientific developments on society;

4. An appreciation of the readiness of the social order to accept and use scientific findings.

Yudkin notes that there are differences in style and emphasis in these accounts, but more striking are the similarities. All the courses are expected to teach some of the facts established by science, to explain the working of the scientific method, and to indicate the place of science in society. But, Yudkin comments, agreement on ends in no way implies agreement on educational means; the content and method of three courses he lists are completely different. Course 'A' centres on human physiology; course 'B' is a superficial survey of chemistry, physics, astronomy, and geology; and course 'C' involves the historical treatment of a few physical and geological topics.

Assuming that pupils and students have little or no previous contact with any scientific disciplines, it is possible to outline the advantages and disadvantages of several different methods for teaching them.

(1) *Survey courses*

Survey courses may range from a superficial study of a particular subject to a more trendy survey of science today or a survey of recent discoveries. The beliefs upon which this type of course are based are, first, that the aim of education in a subject is to provide information on that subject. The second belief, which is closely related to the first, is that the more information is passed on, the better the course will be. The attractions of this type of course seem to be primarily that it can be specifically designed for the non-specialist for whom the course may be his final contact with science in the formal context of education. Again, it no doubt provides a very satisfying outlet for the energetic and enthusiastic teacher, particularly at a grammar school or college. The teacher, who is likely to be taking trouble to keep up with his subject, and through his own interest and curiosity to know about recent advances, no doubt finds it satisfying to pass on this information to his students. Similarly, there is no doubt an attraction to pupils in knowing something about the latest advances in science and being able to impress their friends with titbits of information about the latest gadgetry.

However, survey courses suffer from severe deficiencies. As long ago as 1948, McGrath commented that there was a danger of survey courses teaching the student about science rather than teaching him science. Again, Nowell-Smith (1958, p. 13) has raised a general objection to courses which seek to 'cover the ground'. He comments:

of what conceivable use can it be to learn that there was a man in the seventeenth century whose name was Hobbes and who believed that all men are selfish? Of what interest could this be to any but an intellectual jackdaw? If we set out to give our students birds' eye views we cannot fail to end by giving them bird-like minds. Covering the ground serves no useful purpose ...

In similar vein, Yudkin (1969) castigates survey courses in which the facts are presented and learned by rote. He contrasts this with methods of education where inquiry in science, based on a critical attitude towards evidence, and on an avoidance of the doctrinaire and the authoritarian, is the rule. He notes that while the claim is often made for survey courses that they inculcate 'scientific thinking' the opposite is usually the case.

It is possible that some contact with recent research will stimulate the imagination of students at any level of education, but for a course to be a mere recitation of recently discovered facts is probably damaging. Given a suitable introduction to science, it may be hoped that the student will make use of the abundant paperback literature covering many areas of science in language understandable by the non-scientist. Given the necessary tools of thought, it is even possible that a non-scientist could be equipped to teach himself the complexities of a science in which he was particularly interested and then enjoy studying that science for its own sake later on. He could then provide his own survey, at the level and at the time when he wanted it.

(2) Basic facts and principles courses

Basic facts and principles courses differ from surveys in that they seriously attempt to acquaint the student with some of the principal organizing features upon which a science is based. However, they suffer from the same sort of defects as survey courses. A typical course is described by Reif (1969). Enormous trouble was taken to provide suitable incentives for eminent instructors and professors to take part in the teaching at Berkeley. To quote Reif (op. cit., p. 1033):

... our basic approach has been to select a few themes, basic ideas of great significance, to serve as the structural skeleton of the course. These structural themes, illustrated and elaborated with pertinent facts and examples, are always kept in the forefront. They give coherence to the discussion and facilitate learning by the students. They also help to emphasise that science is more that a collection of observations and gadgets, and that it aims to organise knowledge and to formulate concepts of great generality. In addition, although students are likely to forget most of what they are taught, the few essential themes stressed in the course should linger with them in the years to come.

Although the course of lectures is supported by experimental work in an imaginatively constructed laboratory, there is still the singular danger of teaching concepts as if they were data.

As with survey courses, the basic facts and principles courses are no doubt of great benefit to the teaching staff who have to re-examine at frequent intervals the foundations of the subjects which they teach. They have also the merit noted by Reif that they do not attempt to keep up with the latest gadgetry and do not bewilder the student with detail. But apart from the danger noted above of teaching principles and concepts as though they were data, there is the related problem of knowing which particular facts and principles to cover when the choice is so very large.

(3) *The history or sociology of science*

Barzun (1954) has argued that as science is made by man in the light of his interests, errors, and hopes, just like poetry, philosophy, and human history itself, it is therefore necessary for a student to study the history of science in order to understand the scientific activity. He reports that a man once said to him, 'You don't have to teach the history of science to make a man understand that water is H_2O.' But, Barzun replied, it is precisely what you have to teach unless you are willing to barter understanding for mere voodoo formulae. Conant too in his highly influential book *On understanding science* (1951, first published in 1946) noted the bewilderment of laymen in discussions of science through their not knowing the power and limitations of science and having 'no feel for the tactics and strategy of science'. Conant remarked that (op. cit., p. 26) 'the remedy does not lie in the great dissemination of scientific information among non-scientists. Being well-informed about science is not the same thing as understanding science.'

In an article on the scientific education of the layman Conant (1946, p. 22) wrote:

In my experience, a man who has been a successful investigator in any field of experimental science approaches a problem in pure or applied science, even in an area in which he is quite ignorant, with a special point of view. I designate this point of view 'understanding science'. Note carefully that it is independent of the knowledge of the scientific facts or techniques in the new area to which he comes. Even a highly educated and intelligent citizen without research experience will almost always fail to grasp the essentials in a discussion which takes place amongst scientists concerned with the projected enquiry. This will be so not because of the layman's lack of scientific knowledge or his failure to comprehend the technical jargon of the scientist; it will be to a large degree because of his fundamental ignorance of what science can or cannot accomplish, and his consequent bewilderment in the course of a discussion outlining a plan for a future investigation. He has no 'feel' for the Tactics and Strategy of Science.

Conant went on to argue that there are two ways of probing into complex human activities and their products: the first is to retrace the steps by which certain end results were produced; the second is to dissect the result in the hope of revealing its structural pattern and showing the logical relations of the component parts. Conant believed that for nine people out of ten the historical approach will yield more real understanding of a complex matter. He described the stumbling way in which even the ablest of the early scientists had to fight through thickets of erroneous observations, misleading generalizations, inadequate formulations, and unconscious prejudice (Conant 1946, p. 26). Conventional textbooks on physics, chemistry, biology, or any other of the natural sciences make the whole thing seem very simple, and take no account of these difficulties. In elementary courses students may have to take on faith statements about scientific laws and the structure of matter which are almost as dogmatic as though they were handed down by high priests. The solution Conant proposed was that students should study case-histories in the history of science as students at the Harvard Business School study case-histories from business. Conant selected case-histories which he believed showed the difficulties which attended each new advance in science and the importance of new techniques: how they arose, how they were improved, and how often they revolutionized a field of inquiry. He outlined his criteria for choosing case-histories as follows (1946, p. 33):

1. The field in question must be one in which there can be no doubt that progress has been substantial in the last century or so, and my test would be the imaginary operation of evoking the judgment of the past. 2. This progress must be in terms not of practical achievements or mere amassing of data but in terms of changing concepts and evolving conceptual schemes, the result of experiment or observation, yielding in turn new experiments and observations. 3. One or more of the principles common to the Tactics and Strategy of science must be conveniently illustrated by a study of the case.

Cases devised by Conant and his colleagues have been published in *Harvard case histories in experimental science* (Conant 1957). However, the technique adopted has been criticized by Yudkin (1969, p. 126) on the grounds that the understanding of the tactics and strategy of science that relies on such case-histories is necessarily incomplete.

What is worse, it is incomplete in its most vital part. The moments of discovery are the most important in science: they mark the creation of new concepts or the bringing together of observations in the new pattern. At these times the genius of a great scientist is most notable, and at these times it is most evident that science is more than a structure built by mechanical means alone. An undergraduate whose understanding of science lacks any experience of discovery will have only a skeleton in his grasp.

Yudkin argues that scientific papers, even those used for a case-history, tend to rationalize not only the discoveries but also the progress of a scientific investigation. Published papers usually ignore inconclusive experiments, false starts, and wrong turnings. They are composed with the advantage of hindsight; they are written not to clarify the complex and often irrational progress towards a conclusion but generally describe experiments in a logical, rather than chronological sequence. Yudkin argues that the Conant case-histories, by relying on the writings of scientists, omit the principal part of the scientific activity.

Just as with the survey course, there is a grave danger that the cases become just more information to be learned. Indeed, the principal objection to the historical approach to science is that it is likely to throw unduly heavy emphasis upon the learning of names, dates, discoveries, and so on.

All this is not to deny that studies in the history of science may not do some justice to science as a social institution, as opposed to science as a body of knowledge or an activity. Indeed, courses which while using historical material are sociological in orientation can be explicit in studying science as a social institution. It may be of the utmost importance to understand the conditions which constrain the work of scientists—the prejudices with which they have to battle, the institutional inhibitions on their creativity, the pressure of financial interests on their work, the effect of official secrets acts; or the choice of field generated by some particular personality. However, to study the social conditions in which scientific activity flourishes is not to study science itself.

The history of science or the sociology of science may at first sight appear to be an obvious bridge to the interests and abilities of the student studying an arts subject. Indeed it is difficult to see how anyone seriously interested in science could maintain any perspective upon the value of his work, whether it were 'progressive' or 'retrogressive', without some knowledge of its historical background, and a scientist can hardly afford to be unaware of the sociological context of his work. It does not follow, however, that the best approach for the non-scientist is through the study of the history of science or of the sociology of science.

(4) *The methods and philosophy of science*

Although it has been argued in Chapter 1 that there is no such thing as scientific method, it is possible to identify a common approach of scientists to their material. For example, the 'scientific' procedure may be characterized as follows: a scientist chooses a problem and assembles observations which he thinks are relevant to it; he then proposes an hypothesis to account for his observations; from his hypothesis he makes predictions which can be tested empirically; then he carries out experiments on the basis of his predictions. If the results of his experiments confirm his hypothesis he states it as a 'law'; if the results do not confirm the hypothesis, they may provide a means for modifying it with a view to carrying out further experiments.

It has been argued that the non-scientist can become acquainted with this procedure without the tedium of learning specific facts in a particular subject or of doing boring experimental work. Indeed, much of the value of a scientific education would be lost if justice

D

were not done to the methodological and philosophical foundations of the subject.

Neville (1968) makes a plea for philosophical ideas as the base of science teaching. He notes how arts students often choose their subjects not necessarily because they are pro-arts, but more because they are anti-science. Arts pupils, he suggests, acquire early the impression that their teachers are going to reveal to them absolute truths about the real world. When these 'truths' begin to deteriorate into routine measurements and calculations it is not unreasonable that they become disillusioned. Again, science students have often never questioned the validity of their knowledge. They are convinced that they are Messianic bearers of some absolute truth about the real world, without ever considering to what extent the world is 'real', and whether if there is an absolute truth, it is the business of science to discover it. He comments (op. cit., p. 859), perhaps a little bitterly, that 'it is the pupils who expect to be taught dogmatically who complete the present O- and A-level science courses "satisfactorily", that is, with the most ready acceptance'. Neville bemoans the loss of able and original minds from the science sixth forms, the difficulties in teaching intellectually advanced ideas, and the difficulty of training students in learning techniques. These difficulties, he argues (op. cit., p. 860), all stem from science being taught 'as a means towards self-evident and immutable truths, not, as it should be, from the beginning, as a flexible, intellectual structure of concepts fruitful in expressing and controlling our relationships with our environment.' He argues that if the philosophical implications of science are avoided, confusion results. The terms which are used are not fully apprehended, e.g., 'law'. He takes the concept of 'mass', which has no form, and compares it with 'love', which is also a concept derived from observation of interactions. We can never show 'a love', only show people in love. Similarly we cannot show 'a mass', only something that has mass. He notes the educational damage that is done when a pupil cannot observe in the clear-cut way that his teacher appears to, since he cannot see the mass which he is told is having an effect. He then attributes to himself a sort of 'mass-blindness', and, convinced of his disability, he gives up prematurely his attempt to understand the concept. Neville argues that concepts like that of mass should be tackled as early as possible, as soon as they arise or even before.

But we must note that Neville is arguing for philosophical ideas

to be the base of science teaching in a context in which some
science is carried out. Wisely, he does not argue for concepts to
be taught on their own. The philosophy of science, experience of the
'methods', and articulation of them are best encountered in the
context of some actual study of science.

The major objection to the study of methods and philosophy of
science on their own is that the crucial elements of the scientific
enterprise are once again left out: that is to say, the choice of subject to be studied; the intense imaginative excitement involved in
conceiving an hypothesis; the often breathless frenzy of carrying
out crucial experiments to see whether the hypothesis is correct.
It is perilously easy to teach methods and philosophy of science so
that they become dry and dusty and bypass completely the science
which they serve.

(5) Study of a particular subject in depth

If ideas are the bones of science, particular scientific problems
are the flesh and blood; neither can exist without the other. Probably
the best way to understand what scientists do is to do some science.

This, basically, is what Yudkin (1969) suggests. He argues that
the study of science by the non-scientist undergraduate in particular
must centre on experimental work in the laboratory. With a suitably
controlled mix of experimental work and discussion with tutors, a
student can test hypotheses for himself and, most important of all,
invent hypotheses to account for his own observations. As Yudkin
shows, this can be done with relatively simple apparatus; for
example, some cord and some lumps of metal and wood with
which pendulums can be made. Students could then determine what
are the factors which affect the period of swing. An ordinary stop-
watch would provide sufficiently accurate measurements (Yudkin
1969, pp. 132f.).

An alternative method, also suitable for undergraduates, has been
suggested by Epstein (1970). Essentially Epstein's method involves
the teacher's selecting six to ten original papers within his own
field of research—papers that tell a connected story in some field
of science. These papers are read by the students, who thus share
the intellectual processes of the research as experienced by the
scientist. The papers are discussed in class with emphasis on what
the scientist has done to obtain his results rather than on the facts
discovered. Although this technique does not involve laboratory

practice, if skilfully handled it can clearly avoid some of the pitfalls of the Conant method and at the same time expose students to the ways of thought of practising scientists. Because the technique involves teachers in discussion of papers within their own field of research interest, it has the incidental value of avoiding some of the hazards (described more fully in Chapter 6) of diverting university faculty members from their research. Little preparation is required by the teacher, Epstein argues, for the subject to be discussed is well within his own discipline, and the student is exposed to the excitement of advanced work in the subject he is studying.

However, it is possible to study a particular subject in depth, not by studying within the bounds of a single 'discipline' (which usually means studying a lot of the same thing), but by adopting a topic approach. This was one of the approaches recommended by the Science Masters' Association in their *Report on the teaching of general science* (1950). They suggested as possible topics for study: air, heat, light and oxygen, water, buoyancy and flight, energy, the earth, and applications of science. There is an abundance of questions which could be asked about any one of these topics, and a very wide range of experimental investigations which pupils could carry out for themselves to test hypotheses which they themselves had suggested.

But just as a study of the methods and philosophy of science can be dull without some study of science, so can the study of a science subject become mere routine without some study of its methods and philosophy, and even of its history. In an extremely valuable discussion of the uses of practical work Tricker (1967, pp. 83–4), asks what is the student expected to gain from, for example, a measurement of the acceleration of gravity.

Certainly not a knowledge of its value. It you wanted to know its exact value you would certainly look it up in tables of physical constants. It is to appreciate the limits of accuracy of the measurements from which the results in the tables were taken? There is a point here, but the student's apparatus will be much less accurate than that of the original investigator's and the measurement will probably be carried out in a quite different manner and in a very much shorter space of time. Who wants to know the magnitude of the acceleration of gravity and why do they want to know it? And why measure it by an approximate method? Is the student among the number of those who do want to know its value and does he know why he wants to know it? To what

length should the teacher go in making the apparatus simple to work?
In many cases there is precious little left for the student to do. The
functioning of the apparatus is almost automatic, the student merely
having to make a few motions and connections and observe a pointer
on a scale. These are some of the questions which appear to need consideration.

Tricker goes on to emphasize that for practical work to be
meaningful, it is essential that the student knows why the acceleration of gravity among all the other phenomena of nature has been
singled out for special measurement. If he does not know this, he is
likely to be indulging in measurement for the sake of measurement,
with a corresponding likelihood of his becoming bored. Tricker
attributes the flight of many pupils from the sciences to the arts to
the dampening of interest experienced in making apparently futile
measurements at school. If the study of a particular science subject
is to become the basis for the scientific education of non-specialists,
it is essential that the student should not only be aware of the
reasons for his work but also be enthusiastic about making measurements to test hypotheses. It is for this reason that the sixth approach
to the study of science by non-scientists commends itself.

(6) Science in everyday life: projects

If the objectives in the teaching of science to non-specialists are
to include encouraging the ability to tackle practical problems of
everyday life in a systematic manner and apprehending the organizing principles behind phenomena, it does not particularly matter
where one starts. For the non-specialist, the accumulation of any
given body of information is less important than acquiring the
ability to approach a particular problem in the way most likely to
produce results. If the non-scientist is to be at all characterized by a
'scientific' approach to life, it is desirable that the scientific attitude
pervades his whole way of life. He should be encouraged to apply
scientific imagination to everything with which he comes in contact,
just as any teaching he receives in the humanities encourages detailed observation, and subjective identification with human problems. A profitable approach to the teaching of science to non-
specialists might therefore concentrate upon projects in which
pupils, particularly at the more elementary levels, might be involved,
such as the systematic study of hobbies and other interests. For
example, wireless, aeroplanes, motor-cars and motor-cycles, or

cookery all provide fertile areas for experimental investigation. Tricker (1967, p. 77) has suggested that athletics might provide a fruitful subject for study.

In running, jumping, throwing, the hitting of a ball with a bat, in swimming, diving, riding, balancing and flying, are always to be found some principle or other of dynamics in action. It is probable that the development of the science of dynamics itself was delayed because of the difficulty of obtaining direct experience of movement—particularly of violent acceleration—and to obtain some direct experience can be of the utmost assistance in studying the subject.

He also suggests (Tricker 1967, p. 109) that gardening can be a suitable field for study.

Garden lore, like weather lore, is a very fertile source of elementary problems for investigation. Rules of cultivation have often, in the past, been enunciated on the basis of inadequate experience and many unfounded beliefs survive. Experiments on the effect of the spacing of plants on their growth and productivity, on the effect of depth of planting and germination and survival, or on the effect of different methods of cultivation, are within the grasp of quite ordinary pupils, and those interested in gardening can readily see the importance of them. ... Time of sowing is another possible topic for enquiry, and this will need to be correlated with a record of the weather. Quantitative results may well be the object of many of these experiments. What happens when the recommended steps are not taken and what is the effect on the yield? Does disaster follow, and if so how serious is it?

Under imaginative supervision, a child could suggest a wide variety of hypotheses to be tested, and could have the excitement of suggesting relatively simple experimental techniques which could be used to test his hypotheses.

(7) *Science and other subjects: integrated approaches / bridge subjects*

Some of the principal methodological and philosophical issues underlying the practice of science appear in their most complex forms in the social sciences. In the science education of non-scientists, it may not be necessary to concentrate on the physical sciences. Psychology, social psychology, sociology, anthropology, or geography all involve the hypothetico-deductive method of testing hypotheses against experience. The techniques of measurement used in these subjects, by virtue of their very uncertainty, are often highly suitable subjects for a non-scientist to examine.

One great disadvantage of the social sciences is that first-hand information is more difficult to obtain. It is easy to demonstrate—or better still to let a child discover—some of the fundamental principles which underlie the behaviour of physical phenomena by devising experiments with pieces of string and sealing-wax. Simple experiments in psychology can be devised, but in sociology, anthropology, or geography, for example, the testing of hypotheses requires second-hand material or rather elaborate field-work for which time may not be available.

2.3. The backwash effect of examinations

Any method of teaching requires assessment. Basically, there are three objectives of assessment: first to evaluate the course—mainly for the benefit of the teacher so that he may see if he is meeting his objectives; secondly to provide incentive to the student—so that he may see whether or not he is mastering the material he is studying; thirdly, to measure attainment—this being a compromise between the previous two objectives in that the teacher can see whether the student is meeting the *teacher*'s objectives as opposed to any objectives proposed by the pupil. In a fiercely competitive educational situation, it is almost always the third objective which dominates teaching.

Peter Kelly (1969, p. 503) has commented that it may be salutary to remember that the word *curriculum* is derived from *currere*, meaning 'run', and it is related to Latin terms for chariot races (*currus*, chariot). He adds that the image of the curriculum as a sort of race is too near the truth to be humorous.

The prizes are formidable. Prestige and financial reward are the chief ones, and students and their teachers evolve an elaborate felicific calculus to get the best rewards. As long ago as 1943, the authors of the Norwood Report (Ministry of Education 1943) recommended that the School Certificate be dropped and replaced by internal examinations. The report argued (pp. 45–6) that an examination 'is best conducted by the teachers themselves as being those who should know their pupils' work and ought therefore to be those best able to form a judgment on it'. The direction which change should take is therefore sufficiently clear: 'It is towards placing the conduct of the examination in the hands of the teachers;

they alone can best judge the needs of the mass of their pupils and they ought to be the best judges of the success or failure of the methods they employ.'

The recommendation for internal examination has been taken up for the Certificate of Secondary Education, but for the General Certificate of Education which was set up after the Norwood Report, external examination is still the norm. There is now disturbing evidence that the General Certificate of Education at O-level is being used as a preliminary method of selection for university.

Barnard and McCreath (1970) have reported on a project carried out by the University of Essex in association with the Royal Statistical Society on factors influencing the choice of higher education. They quote results from school surveys on subject commitments in the sixth form and below. The subject combinations studied by pupils at G.C.E. O- and A-level and ways in which the schools provide these combinations in their timetables are shown to be a function of the university entry requirements, which are percolating below the sixth form to two years before O-level. Their paper discusses some of the implications of this on the demand for higher education.

Barnard and McCreath note that the Crowther Committee condemned the situation in which four-fifths of the boys had virtually chosen their sixth-form course, if any, by the age of thirteen or fourteen. The Robbins Committee produced evidence that 40 per cent of university arts students had no science at O-level and over one-third of the science students had no history or geography. After presenting some of the statistical evidence, Barnard and McCreath make the comment (p. 388):

The beginnings of the main University paths may be discerned at entry to secondary education since the first requirement is that pupils should set out on courses which do not at that stage preclude them from attempting at 'O' level the core of subjects from which dominant three 'A' level groups later arise. Over the years to the 'O' level examination, and especially two years before it, the pupils are exposed to certain subject options which, in part, reflect their ability. The resulting curriculum patterns are linked to dominant three 'A' level combinations. Even if there has been a fairly basic core of subjects up to about age thirteen, some diversification and selection is inevitable: diversification because subject boundaries are beginning to be drawn differently, for example 'science' will be separating out into physics, chemistry and biology, and 'English' into language and literature; selection because between 31 and 56 'O' level subjects were offered by each of the different examining boards when the surveys took place and there is a limit to the number which can be tackled by any pupil, however able. Most of the timetable, apart from periods for physical education, will be taken up by subjects in which the pupil will later be expected to reach 'O' level standard.

From questions to upper sixth-formers who had left school, it emerged that half of these pupils considered commitments at age 13–14 were too early and very bad or entirely disadvantageous. The main reasons the former pupils gave were that they did not know their own minds or that a general education was important. About half of them would have made some change in their A-level subjects if starting again, but few would have changed completely. Barnard and McCreath question whether it is desirable in the interests of all sixth-formers that university entry requirements should so dominate the curriculum. They ask if the schools' real, not apparent, freedom to plan their curricula is increasing or decreasing with the fragmentation of subjects at O- and A-level. They ask where does the responsibility lie to convey implications to pupils at the time when they are making commitment to subjects. They ask how long can A-level continue to serve as both a qualifying and a competitive examination for university entrance. The impact on the content and quality of education is, as they see it, serious (Barnard and McCreath 1970, p. 391):

As long as the numbers of qualified applicants coming forward exceed the number of places or jobs which are available and the university, college, training school, or employer is able to exercise a selection procedure which yields sufficient entrants both qualitatively and quantitatively, then there will be no pressure from above to alter a school system which is, in fact, providing for immediate needs. The danger in such a state is that fundamental education issues are scarcely discussed. In recent years serious imbalances in the system have suddenly set up pressures towards change which have raised such issues. When the shortage of candidates for undergraduate places in science and technology first became apparent it was regarded as a scientists' problem to be solved primarily by scientists and engineers and not really impinging significantly on other parts of the education system. But the Council for Scientific Policy received an *education* report from the Dainton Committee since it found it impossible to stay within its strictly science terms of reference. Criticism has been levelled at its competence to deal with the wider sphere but the fact remains that education issues are now being discussed mainly through the initiative of scientists and engineers. There is a real need for those concerned with the arts and social studies subjects to contribute their views though it would be difficult to persuade the majority that there are fundamental issues to discuss as long as the supply of candidates for undergraduate places in these faculties remains embarrassingly buoyant.

Apart from the danger of examinations penetrating the educational system purely as measures of attainment, and thus perhaps becoming ends in themselves, there is the related danger of wrong emphasis in the content of the examinations. Toulmin (1963) noted that skills and factual knowledge are easy enough to test by a written examination, and performance can be numerically graded. Understanding and critical ability, however, call for a more discriminating type of examination, and do not lend themselves so readily to numerical grading. He criticized the G.C.E. examinations on the grounds that they had become almost entirely tests of formal skills, capacities, and abilities, as contrasted with a deeper intellectual grasp and powers of expression. Toulmin attributed the present fragmentation of our culture to the G.C.E. system being geared-up to tests for skills and factual knowledge rather than for understanding and grasp of general ideas. He laid the burden of dealing with the situation firmly at the door of the Matriculation Boards (p. 34):

More is at stake in this problem than mere scholastic organisation. For the future of our science, and of much else, will depend on the intellectual attitudes of the next two generations. Already ... the Athenian attitudes of mind, whose critical probing and speculative freedom have been the stimulus of scientific growth both in the Ancient World and since the Renaissance, are under heavy pressure from the Alexandrian forces of the mid-twentieth-century. ... If the Athenian elements in our science and culture were finally to be overmastered by the Alexandrian elements, which are very strong today, that would indeed be the onset of a new Dark Ages.

3 *Science in Primary Education*

To attempt in 1972 a definitive description of the educational system in England and Wales would be as futile as to try and describe a range of sandhills during a gale. Not only is the structure of the primary, secondary, and tertiary (further and higher) education changing rapidly, but so also is the content of education at each of these stages through various types of curriculum reform.

The following chapters will not attempt to provide a comprehensive survey of science as it is taught to non-scientists throughout the educational system. Instead, they will describe practice in a few sectors of the educational system and will examine the constraints which prevail. No mention will be made of teaching in technical colleges, colleges of further education, teacher-training colleges, polytechnics, adult education or extra-mural departments, or other institutions concerned with the education of non-scientists. These are important sectors of the educational system, but in the present study it should suffice to examine selected examples. Clearly, success at any level of the educational system will depend upon the interests, ability, and initiative of teachers and taught; it will also depend upon the facilities available.

3.1. The place of science in the primary school

Whether one takes the view that the purpose of education is to tame the natural, savage instincts of children, or that it is to lead forth their innate capabilities, its obvious purpose is to fit children for the society in which they will grow up. Reviewing the aims of primary education, the Plowden Committee (Central Advisory Council for Education 1967, para. 505) made the following statement:

A school is not merely a teaching shop, it must transmit values and attitudes. It is a community in which children learn to live first and foremost as children and not as future adults. In family life children learn to live with people of all ages. The school sets out deliberately to devise the right environment for children, to allow them to be themselves and to develop in the way and at the pace appropriate to them. It tries to equalize opportunities and to compensate for handicaps. It lays special stress on individual discovery, on first hand experience and on opportunities for creative work. It insists that knowledge does not fall into neatly separate compartments and that work and play are not opposite but complementary. A child brought up in such an atmosphere at all stages of his education has some hope of becoming a balanced and mature adult and of being able to live in, to contribute to, and to look critically at the society of which he forms a part.

Where in this community of children does science fit in? Discussing the place of science in the primary school (British Association 1961), Nathan Isaacs commented that science is not a single subject at all. There are quite different sciences, each representing a specialized study of some one particular aspect of the world; so that if by 'science' we mean the unified sum of the separate sciences, then it is something that no one can dream of introducing into our primary or secondary schools—or anywhere else. As a subject, he noted, 'general science' can no longer be considered educative. If, however, science is considered, not as a subject but as experience of that type of knowledge of the physical world that can be achieved by systematic investigation, then we are referring to the root and core of all individual sciences. Such experience can be attained. Indeed, Isaacs says that there is no question of bringing science into the junior school; our only concern is to see that it is no longer shut out. The type of experience Isaacs speaks of is that of direct contact with the natural world. The ultimate authority of science rests upon direct observation, experience of, and experiment with the natural world; and experience and experiment are open to even the youngest children.

There is no difficulty in finding starting-points for scientific inquiry in the primary school. As parents are often painfully aware, children are continually asking questions. As long ago as 1946, Rallison demonstrated the keen interest of children in questions of scientific interest. In Rallison's investigation, 1659 boys produced 18 049 questions which would require a knowledge and training in science for an adequate answer; only 4931 of their questions involved other fields of knowledge. Among girls, there was also a well-marked interest in science, but it seemed to be less intense than with the boys: 1855 girls asked 9371 questions for which the explanation came within the field of science, and 12 333 which needed knowledge not drawn from the region of science, to afford a solution. Rallison's report shows how questions are distributed by age, sex, and size of town. However, it is the range of questions which is most impressive. Here is a sample: How does hair grow? How do we breathe? How do eyes work? Why are flowers coloured? How does a wireless work? What causes thunder and lightning? How is paper made? Why is the sea salty? How does a fire burn? How does a steel ship float? Why do glasses magnify? What are stars? How is rain caused? How does water freeze? What causes earthquakes? How was the earth made? How does the gramophone work?

Clearly, many of these topics are far too complex to be tackled in the primary school. But with the teacher's judicious help, children's own questions can provide the best possible starting point for genuinely scientific inquiry. In *Science in primary schools* (Department of Education and Science 1961, p. 9), an example is given of the way in which an inquiry can originate from children's questions. When the solution to a particular problem is felt by children to be urgent, necessity can indeed be the mother of invention:

An example of this arose during a class visit to the sea-shore, when a pupil asked: 'Is it possible to get fresh water from the sea?' The teacher posed this question to the class as a whole and they planned how, either individually or in small groups, they would try to answer it. Six girls decided to sieve the water and after discussing the best size of mesh they selected a piece of muslin. The majority decided that they would try filtering, for they had recently been filtering some muddy water. A few claimed that if they boiled the water the salt would stick to the container, like fur to a kettle, and the water would then be fresh. All these methods were tried and found to be uneffective and the class set out to devise alternative experiments. Two or three children hit on a successful method, suggesting that the salt water be boiled and the "steam" collected from a cold plate held in its path. Here the teacher had turned a useful question to good account, and by patiently letting them speculate and experiment, though knowing that most of the experiments would prove unfruitful, gave them an excellent experience of a method of scientific enquiry.

This type of inquiry is fully in line with the working hypotheses of the National Froebel Foundation about the conditions in which children learn most effectively. In *Children learning through scientific interests* (1968, p. 8) the Foundation suggested that children learn most effectively when the following three conditions are fulfilled:

1. Where they themselves want to know: i.e. to secure the answers to questions originated by them—to find out more about something that has aroused their interest—to solve problems and to discover causes and explanations;

2. Where they enjoy the stimulus of free discussion among themselves, with the teacher acting as helper and pathfinder, and not either as an Army instructor or an oracle;

3. When they have the chance of actively seeking out their own answers, and—with the aid only of queries or suggestions, pointers or hints from the teacher—can experience the thrill of making their own discoveries.

The Foundation pointed out that this view of learning contradicts the traditional approach to teaching, which is often synonymous with instruction.

3.2. Opportunities in the primary school

The teacher in a primary school is blessedly free from the constraints which an examination with its attendant curriculum imposes. He could therefore afford to pay more attention to the hypothetico-deductive approach of science than to the information which results from this approach. Indeed, the flexibility of the primary school situation is one in which the true scientific spirit can probably flourish better than anywhere else in the educational system.

One aspect of this freedom is the freedom to examine a topic when it comes up as a matter of interest for children. The teacher of a mixed class of children of seven and over reported one such occasion (National Froebel Foundation 1966, p. 39):

A boy coming in one very wet afternoon with wet shoes, socks and feet triggered off a question, 'why are his feet wet, and mine are dry?' Many suggestions were given, but the fact that those with dry feet (or the majority anyway) had worn wellingtons eluded even the brighter children. Experiments pouring water over many different kinds of material, e.g. lace, linen, rubber, cotton, plastic, wellington, leather, proved most successful. The whole class joined in, the wet socks had been put on the warm radiator to dry and a girl observed that they were 'smoking'. This caused much discussion between the 'steamers', and the 'smokers'. 'What makes steam?' 'Where does it go?' 'Does it vanish?' Several experiments were done on evaporation.

Although such opportunities are, according to most authorities, always to be seized, there is still a place for a syllabus though not necessarily a rigid one. A syllabus can give a full and clear statement of aims and methods, and some pointers to work throughout the school which would avoid needless repetition and which would ensure that teaching was progressive. A syllabus would probably reveal the special interests of the teacher and would certainly reflect the school's particular environment, but a syllabus can be regarded as a general guide rather than as a directive (Department of Education and Science 1961, p. 14).

The second type of freedom of science in primary education is that of intermingling with other subjects. The Plowden Committee (Central Advisory Council for Education 1967, para. 675) noted how a visit to a stream with the avowed object of collecting specimens may lead to non-scientific consequences—to a poem, or a painting, or to drawings which may be at once accurately observed and artistically pleasing. They note how a visit to a church with history and religion in mind once resulted in a decision by the children to find out how the church was built, what were the engineering problems involved and, surprisingly, how much it weighed! This project involved much careful planning and hard work in mathematics and science, and a great deal of speaking, reading, and writing. The Plowden Committee applauded this type of project because it reflects not only the nature of young children and their methods of learning but also interconnections of subjects which have been more or less arbitrarily classified.

Although it is not necessary for science to involve any mathematics, mathematics is one of the most obvious subjects with which science overlaps. In *Mathematics in primary schools*, the Schools Council (1966) described mathematics as the discovery of relationships. It is in the discovery of relationships that science and mathematics are linked, not only in primary school but also at the most advanced level. Scientists may use mathematics as shorthand; primary school children will use numbers and the relationships be-

tween numbers, shapes, and so on as one way of testing their environment. Observation, as the Schools Council *Bulletin* points
out (p. 89), is different from mere aimless looking. It is undertaken
to discover something unknown; it is looking with a purpose, a
purpose stimulated by questions. Frequently observations involve
measurements of some kind. In the recording of measurements, the
arranging and ordering of results and their interpretation, children
experience mathematics at work. In collecting results of their experiments, assessing their validity and interpreting them, children may
need to tabulate the results, draw a graph, or find the average of a
series of experimental results. In all these activities, children have
first-hand experience of the relationship between mathematics and
science.

Mathematics in primary schools describes how some ten-year-
olds found the relationship between the weight of a collection of
stones and their volume. It was the children's own idea to find
the volume of the stones by completely filling a bucket with water.
They then stood the bucket in a basin and carefully lowered each
large stone in turn into the water, catching the overflowing water in
the basin; this they measured in a measuring jug. The same group of
children were asked if they could find how many times as heavy
as water a large stone was. It was their own idea to weigh the
water which overflowed when the stone was carefully lowered into
the water. They compared the weight of the stone with the weight
of the water it displaced and found that the stone was about three
times as heavy as water (p. 90).

Just as a scientific 'discovery' may be an aspect of measuring, so
in the primary school measuring may be an aspect of another subject
such as geography; distances can be measured on a globe with
pieces of string and the distances compared one with the other.
Again, meteorology as an aspect of geography is one favourite
method of introducing primary school children to scientific concepts
and practices and also to the fabrication of simple bar-charts or
graphs. But the important point underlying these observations is
the one made in *Science in primary schools* (Department of Education and Science 1961, pp. 26–7), that to the primary school child
knowledge need not be subdivided into subjects. Geography, history, literature, mathematics, and science may at any time overlap,
one fact throwing light on another; and they all remain very much
in the province of the class teacher. The pamphlet points out that

the scientific qualities to be cultivated in the primary school are ones which children already possess to a large degree—curiosity, acuteness of observation, a desire to experiment, to collect, and to sort. The best teacher of science at this stage, therefore, is not always the science expert, but often the good class teacher with an interest in the subject who himself wants to know more. Ennever, director of the Nuffield Science 5/13 project, has noted that in primary schools education is child-centred. In secondary schools, education becomes subject-centred, and the teachers are severely restricted by the syllabus. However, as Ennever has pointed out in the Schools Council *Working Paper Number 22* (1969b, p. 61), whatever degree of permissiveness is possible in studies in the primary school, the teaching will still be subject to the discipline of good educational principles.

The children will not, as one critic implied, simply be left in a room to discover Newton's laws on their own. They will plan their work both on their own and with their teacher, who, doubtless armed by foresight, will already have made some preparation. What they learn through these studies they should be clear about, but if they are in small groups, or if the work is individual, it will be no easy matter for the teacher to plan effective means for this to be achieved. Group and class discussions will draw threads together and written records help to crystallize knowledge, but the unobtrusive supervision of much diversity will remain a skilled business and a key activity.

Although the relatively unstructured encouragement of exploration of the primary school may be said to have many of the advantages of the genuinely scientific enterprise, it has been objected, particularly by teachers of science in secondary schools, that children come to them possessing all kinds of fragmentary, unclassified information, some of it inaccurate and all of it incomplete. Indeed, it seems to be a characteristic of scientific education that this criticism is almost always levelled at any section of the educational process by the section above it. However, the Plowden Committee commented (para. 673) that

knowledge is always incomplete, and it is only gradually that children can build up a coherent understanding of any aspect of it. The kinds of classification that are useful and necessary at an advanced stage may be meaningless at the age of eleven. If children leave their primary schools with their natural curiosity not only unimpaired but sharpened, with experience of first-hand discovery in several different fields, the sum idea

E

of what questions to ask and how to find the answers, they will be well equipped to proceed with a scientific education.

One might add that children who learn the habit of following their curiosity where it leads them, regardless of subject boundaries, and carrying out practical tests of phenomena whenever possible, will already have taken the first step in participating fully in science culture.

4 Science in Secondary Education: Up to the Sixth Form

THE principal constraints on science education in the primary school result from the abilities of pupils and of teachers; in the secondary schools the picture is very different. Here the effects of examinations make themselves felt, and assessment of the science teaching is usually assessment of the attainment of pupils rather than assessment of the effectiveness of teaching. If culture is the reaction to and handling of environment by groups of people, and if education is the transmission of culture, it is not unreasonable that the primary purpose of education should be to equip the individual to live in his society. The unfortunate fact is that, for a variety of reasons, examinations have to a large extent become ends in themselves, a sort of currency with which individuals can buy themselves into good jobs. It is then only too easy for subjects to be taught with the sole purpose of getting pupils through examinations, to the neglect of the cultural values the subjects contain. To a large extent, this chapter will be a discussion of the constraints imposed upon science education for non-specialists by the examinations which the majority of non-specialists take.

We shall first consider the development of the Certificate of Secondary Education (C.S.E.), and then the General Certificate of Education O-level. Although the G.C.E. O-level was devised well before the C.S.E., less than half of the leavers from secondary schools take any subjects at the G.C.E. O-level at all; whereas, since C.S.E. was introduced in 1965, its popularity has been rapidly growing in the schools, and now well over 200 000 pupils a year take it.

41. The Certificate of Secondary Education

One of the fourteen regional examining bodies of the Certificate of Secondary Education (the West Yorkshire and Lindsey) issues a pamphlet about C.S.E. to parents. It explains that the examination is recognized by the Department of Education and Science, and that 'in this respect it can be compared to the G.C.E.'. The pamphlet goes on:

> Although external papers will be available, the C.S.E. breaks new ground: schools can suggest to the Board the work on which they wish pupils to be assessed; they can even ask for assessment to be based on the results of their own internal tests. In addition ... the quality of the work of each pupil will not be judged on written papers alone: the opinion of the class teacher, his work during the course, the skill of his hands, the way in which he can talk about the subject and any personal researches he carries out, may all be taken into account.

Unlike the G.C.E., the C.S.E. is a child-oriented, teacher-controlled examination. An air of experiment still hangs about it. How and why did it come into being, what is it, and what sort of science curriculum and examinations does it provide? It is valuable to examine these questions to discover the extent to which the C.S.E. can contribute to the science education of non-specialists. (For a detailed study of the C.S.E. see Whalley 1969.)

External examinations had first been set up on a national scale in 1917 with the creation of the School Certificate and the Higher School Certificate. The School Certificate examinations had to be passed in one of three groups: English, history, etc.; languages; science and maths. Dissatisfaction with the School Certificate arrangements led to a report by the Spens Committee (Board of Education 1938), which noted that its witnesses thought: 'That despite all safeguards, the School Certificate Examination ... now dominates the work of the schools, controlling both the framework and the context of the curriculum.' Later, the Norwood Committee (Ministry of Education 1943) of the Secondary Schools Examination Council (or S.S.E.C. as it was known until it became the Schools Council) issued a report condemning the School Certificate and recommending a scheme to replace it: an internal examination, teacher-controlled, and, indeed, much resembling the C.S.E. that was later to emerge. The Norwood Committee Report, however, recommended that for a transitional period of seven years there should be a single-subject external examination. This was to be the General Certificate of Education, which was introduced in 1951. However, it was never intended that the General Certificate of Education should be the sole examination for secondary education. With the increase in school population following the raising of the school-leaving age in the 1944 Education Act, it was found in the 1950s that a growing number of pupils and parents were demanding some sort of leaving certificate other than the G.C.E., which was academic and aimed at the top 20 per cent of the age-groups. The pressure for a new type of examination was seen by the growth of local external examinations. By 1959, about one-third of all G.C.E. O-level entries were from schools other than grammar schools, and the power of the eight national examining boards was growing.

In 1958, the Ministry of Education appointed the Secondary Schools Examination Council to look into the question of examinations other than the G.C.E. The S.S.E.C. had been responsible since its formation in 1917 for the maintenance of standards among the bodies that conducted public examinations. It produced its report, known as the Beloe Report, in 1960. The Committee's terms of reference were 'to review current arrangements for the examination of Secondary school pupils other than by G.C.E., and to consider what developments are desirable, and to advise the Council whether and if so, what, examinations should be encouraged or introduced and at what ages and levels' (Ministry of Education 1960, p. 1). The Beloe Committee reported that, in looking at examinations other than the G.C.E., 'we have found much that caused us misgiving, and some features that caused grave disquiet' (para. 56). The three main causes for concern were: the uneven marking between the examination boards; the narrow questions set in the exams—'too predominantly of a kind that calls only for memorized facts and opinions, rather than eliciting the pupils' interest, imagination or comment from direct experience' (para. 58); and the lack in many of the papers of a 'distinctive aim of their own'.

The Beloe Report recommended the introduction of new examinations, which it was hoped would supersede all existing examinations below the G.C.E. O-level. These examinations would be appropriate for pupils at the end of the fifth year of a secondary school course, and would be designed for the pupils in the ability range concerned rather than providing replicas of the G.C.E. but at a lower level.

In 1961 the Minister of Education accepted the examination proposed by the Beloe Report, and the S.S.E.C. set up a Standing Committee to work out the details. The S.S.E.C.'s seventh report (Ministry of Education 1963) was issued as a result, defining the scope and standards of the proposed C.S.E. It was established that the new examination should be organized regionally, that it should not be a pass–fail examination, and that it should contain three methods, or modes, of examining, from which the school could choose. This basis of choice makes the C.S E., in theory at least, a very flexible form of examination.

The three modes of the C.S.E. are :

Mode I: An examination that is set and examined by the board, usually with a solid proportion of just written answers;

Mode II: An examination that is set by the school in that it submits its curriculum and plans the course, but the board examines;

Mode III: An examination that is both planned and carried out fully by the school, with 'moderation' only from the board.

The Report proclaimed that the C.S.E. was designed for a band of candidates extending from those who just overlapped the group taking G.C.E. O-level to those who are just below the average in ability, that is, the lower 80 per cent of the ability group, or so this is commonly assumed for ease of division.

The C.S.E. is very much the child of the Schools Council, which does research into curriculum development and issues examination bulletins as guidance for the C.S.E. boards. The Schools Council, with its massive programme of projects up and down the country, has certainly given the C.S.E. a status it might otherwise have lacked if, for example, only the local education authorities had been made responsible for the examination. From the outset, it was the intention that the outstanding characteristic of the C.S.E. should be freshness and vitality, and that the examinations would reflect and not inhibit the originality of the work being done in the schools. As the *Examination Bulletin* No. 1 (Schools Council 1963) put it: 'Effective teacher control of syllabus content, examination papers, and examining techniques is the rock on which the C.S.E. system will stand.'

The Schools Council has been very active in finding ways to monitor the standards of the C.S.E. On behalf of the Schools Council, the National Foundation for Educational Research has carried out an item analysis and reliability study, which looks into the details of the C.S.E. scripts and questions, and analyses the question content; a content validity study, which examines the statements of educational objectives, based on Bloom's taxonomy, of syllabus content and aims; and a meaning-of-grade study, to discover what each grade indicates about the response of the pupil, and what it can indicate if the papers are replanned. The National Foundation for Educational Research acts as consultant to the boards as well on individual problems.

The first *Examination Bulletin* (Schools Council 1963, p. 81) outlined the aims of science in C.S.E.:

> Because the pupils who will take C.S.E. will live in a civilization increasingly dependent upon science, their education should give them as much understanding of its principles as they are capable of gaining within the time available. They are not likely to become research scientists or technologists and many of them will find employment which will not require deep understanding of science; yet they all need, for their own and their community's sake, some knowledge of the content of the various fields of science, of discoveries and the way major applications have followed. But a knowledge of facts is not enough. No less important, their study should bring the pupils to appreciate the methods which scientists have found successful, and the strength and limitations of these methods.

The *Bulletin* gives an example (p. 86) of a science question from the C.S.E. Like many of the questions, it deals with the ability of the pupil to design experiments.

If you tie a piece of rubber to the end of a strong but thin string and spin it above your head, keeping the rubber in a horizontal circle, the string becomes taut. When you double the rate of spinning, is the tension doubled? Suggest a way in which this might be examined by an experiment. When the astronauts travelled round the earth they moved very nearly in a circle. Why was no pulling string needed then?

Science subjects are usually popular. For example, in 1966, 45 per cent of the total subjects taken at C.S.E. were scientific and technical. The C.S.E. boards have designed many different types of questions in science papers. The open layout and simple diagrams emphasize understanding of principles as opposed to rote memorization of facts. For example, one question gave a diagram showing the reflection of a man shaving. The question asked whether the man was using his right or his left hand. Another question showed a diagram of a car and near it a small truck bearing a load. The rubric explained that the figure represented a car travelling at 40 mile/h. The cars hits the stationary small truck. The driver of the car is not wearing a seat-belt. The questions were, 'State briefly what will happen to the driver's body at the moment of impact. In the truck there is a tall unstable load. Will the load fall forward or backwards?'

Other questions (also taken from the East Anglian Examinations Board Mode I examinations) demand a similar level of under- standing. For example, the following questions on heat could not be answered by a simple rote recitation of formulae:

Give a scientific explanation for each of the following statements

(a) A thick glass tumbler is likely to crack when hot water is poured into it although a thin glass tumbler may not when so treated.
(b) When the volume of a fixed mass of gas is decreased the pressure is increased even though the temperature remains constant.
(c) You feel warm when wearing a dry bathing-costume but feel cold when the costume becomes wet.
(d) When heat is supplied to melting ice the temperature of the mixture does not rise until all the ice has melted.
(e) There is no change in the reading of a clinical thermometer when it is removed from the patient's mouth.
(f) Food cooks more quickly in a pressure cooker than in an open saucepan.

A welcome feature of these questions is that they relate the principles of physics to everyday living.

Subject integration in C.S.E.

In the last chapter, the interdisciplinary nature of primary school education was noted as being an eminently satisfactory way of inte- grating 'scientific' studies with other studies. An admirable feature of the C.S.E. is that it can follow up the possibilities available in primary school science. All the C.S.E. boards are experimenting with interdisciplinary courses. Their opportunity is much greater than that of the G.C.E. boards because with Mode III examinations any school can build up a course on the resources and interests it has in the school at the time and use it for the C.S.E. Robert Sibson, a Joint Secretary of the Schools Council, has noted that Mode III examinations grew from 8·9 per cent of the total subject entry in 1966 to 10·7 per cent in 1968. 'One of the developments which has emerged as C.S.E. has grown is that of integrated courses comprising contributions from two or more of the traditional subject areas ... the Council is encouraging the boards to increase the common stock of experience by experiment and observation' (Sibson 1969, pp. 12–13).

However, as was mentioned in *C.S.E.—an assessment of progress* (Leeds University Institute of Education 1968), the use of Mode III varies a lot between boards, and this has been the cause of some concern. In 1967, for example, whereas Mode II examining formed 50 per cent of the total examining in the West Yorkshire and Lindsey Board and the J.M.B., in the Welsh Joint Board and the North West Examining Board, 99 per cent of the examining was Mode I. Indeed, only four of the fourteen boards had a greater percentage than 15 per cent in Mode III (p. 27). It was found that the stress on Mode I tended to occur mostly in dense city areas: 'One can only hazard a guess that in such places each school is fighting for its own catchment area, there is a battle to produce the best external exam results, and therefore an emphasis on the coaching and cramming which can so easily go along with Mode I' (p. 34).

There is clearly a danger of C.S.E. becoming just another second-class cramming hurdle for the secondary school pupil. However, the Mode III method of examining has considerable potential if the schools are courageous enough to take it up. As it happens, most of the integrated courses appear to be on the humanities side, but there are increasing numbers of courses which include science. In the West Yorkshire and Lindsey Regional Examining Board, some schools are offering courses called, for example, 'Science and Mankind', 'Physiology and hygiene', 'Modern studies'. One of the Board's schools did a C.S.E. on photography. In this examination, which was devised to stimulate a worth-while interest in the art and science of photography, out of a total of 200 marks, 105 went to the theory papers and 95 to photographs produced by the pupils. Another school did a C.S.E. on engineering science. In this, 60 per cent of the marks went to the scientific part of the course—heat, light, materials, etc., 20 per cent to experimental work carried out during the course, and 20 per cent to a project done during the course on, for example, a survey of the motor industry, or a historical survey of technology.

This type of imaginative examination is likely, for a good number of years yet, to be put on only after considerable effort. The G.C.E. still has much greater prestige. It is better known, and it is also known as being designed for the top 20 per cent of the ability in the age-group. The difficulties in mounting C.S.E., particularly in its

Mode III version, are even more acute when there is a clear overlap in ability between G.C.E. and C.S.E. candidates. This overlap has caused some criticism, much as the dreaded 11-plus did. The South Western Examinations Board did a survey in 1965 and 1966 (reported in their Second Annual Report, 1966) among candidates who took both G.C.E. and C.S.E. They found that 37 per cent and 40 per cent of those who passed G.C.E. failed to get grade I of C.S.E., which is supposedly equivalent; and that 81 per cent of the C.S.E. grade I pupils gained G.C.E. They pointed out, however, that several factors made for rather rough correlation of these results, such as the fact that pupils were following two syllabuses at the same time, that C.S.E. was taken at an earlier date than G.C.E., and so on. Nevertheless, while there is a difference in status between the two types of examination, it is inevitable that some candidates should be accorded a lower status than they deserve.

The difference in status is unfortunate, particularly because the examinations differ not only in structure and organization but also in philosophy and aims. A brief summary is, perhaps, appropriate at this point. The main differences are set out in Table 4.1.

C.S.E. came into action in 1965. The year after it began, one head-master reported his reactions, admitting that: 'There are some who would have preferred to have travelled more slowly and delayed the launching for a year' (Bradshaw 1966, pp. 28–31). However, he felt that the C.S.E. promised several clear assets; these included an incentive for children to stay at school, because C.S.E. is essentially a record for those who have followed five years of secondary school-ing; greater employment prospects; and more thought on the course-work and on examinations as a whole. But he already noted the difference in status between C.S.E. and G.C.E. 'If the answer is not to be *no* examinations, then surely it must be *one* examination.'

In March 1970, the National Union of Teachers proposed that G.C.E. and C.S.E. should become one examination, organized on C.S.E. lines. This idea has been much discussed, particularly since when the Standing Committee on University Entrance and the Schools Council produced their proposals for F- and Q-level examinations carefully saying that they did *not* mean 'that C.S.E. or 'O' level would be discontinued' but adding later on that O-level would 'become superfluous as far as entry to full-time higher educa-tion was concerned' (*Proposals for the curricula and examinations in the sixth form*, December 1969, paras 7 and 14).

Since O-level is currently (1971) the academic examination for the top 20 per cent of the ability group, and is used primarily for entry to other parts of the educational system, the G.C.E. boards are understandably not keen to let the G.C.E. O-level disappear. Whatever the fate of C.S.E. and of G.C.E., it is to be hoped that

TABLE 4.1.

Comparison of G.C.E. and C.S.E. examinations

G.C.E.	C.S.E.
(1) Exam intended for top 20%.	(1) Intended for lower 40–80% of age group.
(2) Conducted by eight boards, all operating nationally, some overseas. Schools can choose board.	(2) Conducted by fourteen boards, regionally. Schools take local boards.
(3) Exam is pass–fail.	(3) Results graded, but no pass–fail.
(4) Exams mainly external, syllabuses and marking done by boards.	(4) External examinations available, but boards have to offer facilities for internal assessment.
(5) O-level often used as basis for sixth-form and university entrance and for work.	(5) C.S.E. a leaving certificate, is used less (but increasingly as often) as O-level for work.
(6) No upper age-limit, candidates need not be at school.	(6) Candidates must be at school, must be aged 16, or in the final term of the fifth year of a five-year course of secondary education, or must have completed such a course.
(7) Candidates may re-sit soon after a failure.	(7) Candidates may re-sit the examination (presumably to gain higher grades), and stay at school for it.
(8) Examination not teacher-controlled but there is teacher-participation in it.	(8) Teacher-control basic to C.S.E.
(9) Assessment of course-work a minor feature of G.C.E.	(9) Course-work characteristic of C.S.E., and usually forms an essential part of all assessment.
(10) No provision, or only rarely, for continuous assessment.	(10) Some Mode III examinations are based on continuous assessment.

the Mode III technique of C.S.E. will spread, because through it there would seem to be the greatest chance for the average school-leaver not only to have some effective contact with science but also to see how the 'scientific experience' is related to other types of experience which he may have.

4.2. The General Certificate of Education O-level

If the C.S.E. offers at least some hope of an introduction to science culture for the non-scientist, so too should the G.C.E. However, as G.C.E. is an academic examination, the pressure for it to be subject-oriented is very great. Indeed, it is in the functioning of the G.C.E. O-level that the divisive effects on our culture of our educational system are most readily seen.

It can be said that an examination's function is essentially secondary to the teaching. The teaching comes first, and the examination simply measures the results of the teaching. The first report of the Oxford Delegacy in 1858 (reproduced in part in the report for 1968–9) reflects this attitude:

An examination would give a definite aim to the scholars; and would afford evidence to the public how far the exertions of both have been successful. It was not, however, expected or wished that the university should undertake to prescribe authoritatively any particular course of instruction, or should endeavour in any way to interfere with the system any schoolmaster was pursuing. The university was asked only to test results, not to enquire into methods.

These principles are still followed by the Delegacy.

However, syllabuses tend to become 'examining syllabuses', not 'teaching syllabuses'. It may appear that the examining boards are the grey eminences who set up the syllabuses and provide strait-jackets in which schools wriggle helplessly. The boards exist, however, to examine what is taught not to dictate what is taught. An unfortunate feedback system seems to be set up by which schools seem to teach what is most easily examined—memorizable facts—and examining boards tend to follow what is taught in the questions they offer. The fate of general science is a case in point.

The eight G.C.E. boards usually offer examinations in single-subject sciences (physics, chemistry, biology, etc.) some in double-subject sciences (physics-with-chemistry, chemistry-with-biology, etc.) and in general science. The general science examination was started as a single subject in 1918 as a School Certificate subject to offset the narrow single courses. As Bassey (1963, p. 24) noted, the examination was popular and between 1930 and the 1950s its candidates trebled.

It had started to much acclaim. Sir Richard Gregory (1922),

president of the Educational Science Section of the British Association wrote:

Science should be science for all, and not for embryonic engineers, chemists, or even biologists; it should be science as part of a general education—unspecialised therefore and without reference to prospective occupation or profession, or direct connection with possible university courses which might follow.

In 1933 the British Association published a pamphlet *General science in schools* which asserted (p. 329) that

General Science should be taught in all Secondary schools and on all sides of such schools, in as much as knowledge of General Science forms an essential part of liberal education.

But at the end of the 1950s came a slump in interest in general science (W. S. James 1957, pp. 15–17):

There is no doubt that General Science is a soft option: it has been called cigarette-card knowledge, and it is nothing more than a collection of odds and ends.

The G.C.E. boards now have very few candidates for general science, although some schools take it simply because they lack science staff to cope with single-science examinations. The Oxford Delegacy, for example, offers 'additional General Science' at O-level, and the numbers fell from 819 takers in 1951 to 165 takers in 1968—compared to over 48 000 candidates in English language in 1968. The Joint Matriculation Board is dropping its General Science II, which was originally intended, with General Science I, to form a basis for sixth-form studies. Boards are revising their syllabuses, and yet they are still finding that the numbers taking the new mixed subjects are falling off in preference for the single, specialized O-levels. The Oxford Delegacy of Local Examinations (in their *General Report* for 1968–9, p. 51) discussed the problems associated with their additional general science:

In educational terms at present, any general paper by its very nature, must suffer from a number of disadvantages in the specialist sense ... to the teacher and pupil these are expressed in terms of inferiority and difficulty compared to the advantages of concentrating on a single subject with all its apparent water-tightness, tidiness and opportunity for rote-learning ... but it provides opportunity for a more integrated approach for the teaching of science, and in the transfer of knowledge from one section to another in explanation of natural phenomena ...

All the more cause to lament its sick state.

Whether or not it is true that the traditional G.C.E. O-level in a single-science subject has a straitjacket effect, the important fact is that teachers *think* that this is so. In a discussion on 'The crisis in science teaching in schools' at the Royal Society of Arts (5 March 1969) H. G. Judge stated that 'science in schools is collapsing'. In the discussion following Judge's speech, one member, a head of a science department, said: 'I cannot inculcate a love of science in my children because it is against their interests ... if I encourage my pupils to try to find out the actual facts of chemistry, to find out what nature is all about, then they will be real scientists, but they will fail their exams' (op. cit., p. 434).

Nyholm (1964, pp. 10–11) urged that it is time that we brought our syllabuses up to date and gave teachers a chance to teach science so as to stimulate students rather than satisfy a stereotyped system. In recent years, there has been much discussion of practical work, of objective testing, of project work, and, more recently, of the inclusion in courses of some consideration of science and its impact on society. In this discussion, even Nuffield science (discussed below) has not escaped attack (cf. Gresswell 1970, pp. 528–33). Most of the protest has been about the heavy factual content of G.C.E. O-levels.

Amos (1968, p. 323) found that biology teachers thought that in O-level biology the main emphasis was on imparting information, whereas it should have been, they thought, on the understanding of the scientific method. 'Although teachers adjust their teaching to the believed requirements of the G.C.E., they pursue objectives concerned with scientific enquiry which they consider unlikely to be evaluated in the exams.'

4.3. Science curricula reform: Nuffield science

Examinations and curricula are obviously very closely related. In fact, as noted above, examinations often determine curricula. In parallel with the movements for reform of examinations in the last twenty years have been vigorous attempts to reform curricula. These attempts have taken place not only in the United Kingdom but also in America. Most of the attempts to reform science curricula have been aimed principally at ridding them of the rigid systematic stress on facts; as Kuslan and Stone (1968, p. 2) observed:

Science is built on a foundation of facts and must always seek new facts, but instruction in science of the non-scientist must also strive for goals far nobler than the mere recall of facts and understanding of scientific phenomena ... Science is simultaneously a *kind* of knowledge and a *way* of using and gaining that knowledge.

So great was the stress on rote-learning of facts, that French was led to write (in Cohen and Watson 1952, p. 17): '... if we are honest, we must confess that science education, which once showed such great promise as a liberating study and a new highway to mental discipline, has become only a tortuous technical highway to specialization.'

In the United Kingdom, Best (1955, p. 167) criticized secondary school science: 'The emphasis throughout should be on the activity that leads to discovery rather than on the laws themselves.'

The Crowther Report (Central Advisory Council for Education 1959, para. 385) endorsed the English principle of specialization, or intensive study as it would better be described. However the Report emphasized:

It is the principle that we endorse. If that meant that we had to rest content with some of the practices that are to be observed in English schools at the present time, we might well reverse our view. There are undoubtedly some abuses of specialisation, which ought to be corrected. But the best line of advance, in our opnion, is to reaffirm the principle and reform its application rather than to abandon it altogether.

The Crowther Committee also deplored the tendency to teach the memorization of facts (para. 393).

The complaints against burdens of factual knowledge amount almost to a shriek. In 1960, the Annual Report of the Advisory Council on Scientific Policy (paras. 46, 47) accused the Oxbridge entrance requirements of distorting the science curricula in schools and criticized the state of science education up to O-level:

We have no doubt that school science curricula are in need of a thorough re-examination ... It has been suggested to us that up to 20%–25% of the content of the curricula in physics, chemistry, and biology could be removed without any harm—and indeed with benefit ... We consider that specialisation in schools has gone too far ... All pupils in the middle school should have the same general education in which science should play its full part.

One of the main pressures for reform came from the Science

Masters' Association (now the Association for Science Education), which in 1957 published a policy statement about the place of science subjects in the curriculum. Joint panels of the Association of Women Science Teachers and the Science Masters' Association considered the separate needs of chemistry, biology, and physics, and in 1961 the reports of these panels were published, together with a revised policy statement. The final statement and reports were issued in 1963 after further discussion and experiment. The main recommendations were that all pupils should follow a 'balanced' course of science subjects up to the end of their fifth year. There should be no segregation into arts and science specialists until the pupil had passed beyond this stage; there should be science in both specialist and general studies in the sixth form; and there should be factually-reduced A-level courses. The report outlined three phases of science for secondary schools. The first phase, for the first two years, aimed to maintain and extend the natural interests in science of pupils, and to introduce further laboratory work. This was to be followed by an intermediate phase which would provide an adequate course both for early leavers and for those continuing in science; this intermediate phase would stress more solving of problems 'leading to the formulation of hypotheses'. The third phase was the advanced sixth-form stage both general and specialist.

These proposals were not ignored by the examining bodies; much was incorporated into new syllabuses. But what was needed was not simply new syllabuses, but a complete teaching programme on the lines of that proposed by the American Physical Science Study Committee (cf. Lord and Ritchie 1962). What Warren (1961) wrote about physics was applicable to all sciences:

A radical reform of physics education is urgently required. Although reduction of excess material is vital, little else will be achieved just by introducing new syllabuses since the same ideas will inevitably be taught. What is required is a critical attitude . . .

A new method of teaching was required. To develop a programme similar to that proposed by the American Physical Science Study Committee required resources beyond those available to the Association for Science Education. It was at this point, in December 1961, that the Nuffield Foundation announced that they were going to allot £250 000, later increased to £430 000, to the development of a suitable teaching programme, with £250 000 more for the publica-

tion of books for the three programmes. The first Nuffield programmes were to provide courses in biology, chemistry, and physics
for pupils in the 11–16 age range.

Meanwhile, there was further discussion and more reports from
other quarters, all concerned with the arid condition of science
courses at the time. Her Majesty's Inspectors issued two pamphlets
on current ideas on curricular reform. One of them, *Science in
secondary schools* (Ministry of Education 1960), stressed the need
for imaginative re-thinking of the pre-O-level courses. Bassey (1963)
advocated the introduction of a new subject, scientific studies, which
would examine scientific method, the social context of science, and
so on. As Bassey said, school science is specialist all the way, even
though the majority of those who take it are the 'others' not the
'eggs'. Kerr carried out an investigation sponsored by the Gulbenkian Foundation into the nature and purpose of practical work in
school science. In 1964 he reported teachers' opinions on reasons
for doing practical work: 'to encourage accurate observation, to
promote scientific ways of thinking, and to provide an opportunity
to find out facts and principles by observation'. Kerr (1964, para.
103) reported that 'no aspect of science education is more urgently in
need of attention'.

Hear and forget; see and remember; do and understand. It was
this last maxim which lay behind the Nuffield reforms. What do they
consist of and how successful are they?

The programme sponsored by the Nuffield Foundation aims to
improve the methods of teaching rather than the examinations,
although a reform in examinations will almost inevitably follow if
the scheme is successful because examination boards examine what
schools teach. This is not the place for an extensive review of all the
different activities and experiments undertaken under the aegis of
the Nuffield Foundation, but it is worth examining some of the
objectives of Nuffield science and seeing what kinds of problems
constrain those who are trying out the programme.

The principles of the Nuffield physics programme have been outlined by John Lewis (1965, p. 85) as follows:

(a) A physics programme should be complete in itself. (b) It should build
on the natural curiosity of the child. (c) It should be relevant to the
world outside the classroom. (d) It should give a broad picture of what
modern science is about, and the way scientists think. (e) It should not

F

contain too much material but should contain a few ideas which the child can make his own. (f) It should strive for understanding. (g) It should foster a spirit of enquiry.

The basis of the Nuffield physics programme is the simple empirical approach in which pupils do most of the practical work, with the teacher adopting the role of adviser rather than of instructor. The emphasis is clearly on principles of inquiry, not on the learning of facts.

The advantages of this type of approach need no emphasis; however there are clearly snags in the scheme, which in physics involves a great amount of equipment and experiment. O'Donnell (*in* Bainbridge 1969, p. 53) describes some of the difficulties in the survey of the Northumberland trials. The role of the teacher in Nuffield physics is much more subtle than before and it is sometimes difficult to maintain order and a sense of purpose in a class who are finding things out for themselves:

'This is particularly true of what the Nuffield course calls 'open-ended experiments', where no obvious scientific truth has been exposed. In Year 1 for instance, pupils have little see-saws on which they place piles of small brass weights, always keeping them balanced. Very few reach the 'lever law' on their own. The teacher feels he ought to tell the others: 'Not yet,' says the book.

The maximum number of pupils considered suitable for a class of Nuffield physics is thirty-two. Problems of overcrowding create enormous chaos and difficulties, as in any programme involving extensive experimental work by pupils. The sheer difficulty of supervising a large number of children is formidable when the temptations to flick pellets with pieces of elastic, or to bounce brass weights up and down on springs and fling them into the air is almost irresistible. Another problem is that of the difficulty of ascertaining how much each child has understood, which ones are idling, and how much it matters if some are behind in the experiments. The questions the pupils are trying to answer are searching and the teaching is strenuous. But successes have been recorded. O'Donnell, for example, states (op. cit., p. 50) 'on reflection the testing of the Nuffield physics was exhausting but interesting and worthwhile ... It is now quite common to hear a first year child talk about gas pressure in terms of molecular motion and a second year pupil describe the behaviour of an electron beam and a cathode ray oscilloscope ...'

Nuffield chemistry similarly lays emphasis on finding out. The scheme consists of three stages:

(1) Exploration of materials, with emphasis on the practical rather than on the theoretical.

(2) Using ideas about atoms and particles, with emphasis on the use of the imagination and the acquisition by the pupils of some simple but useful concepts.

(3) A more advanced stage with optional topics for investigation.

The first two of these stages by themselves can act as a basis for the C.S.E. Although there is a great deal of practical work it is used to illustrate basic theoretical principles. Some of the experiments can be quite dramatic, as W. Garfitt explains (*in* Bainbridge 1969, pp. 38f.). He describes the work on 'Topic 21' on the breaking down and building up of large molecules. The greatest delight he notes (p. 41) was had from the making of nylon.

The lesson reached its climax with the whole class tramping in single file around the laboratory, producing a seemingly endless strand of nylon from a 100 ml beaker containing an aqueous solution of hexamethylene diamine and using a solution of Adypyl chloride in carbon tetrachloride. Yes, it must be admitted that Nuffield chemistry lessons are often somewhat noisier than traditional type lessons, but the noise is markedly purposeful.

Peter Kelly of the Nuffield Biology Project team has outlined how interest in biology has increased dramatically in recent years both in Britain and in the U.S.A. (Kelly 1967). Biology, he says, is often looked upon as the cultural science at O-level. Certainly if the number of candidates for science subjects in the summer examinations of the School Certificates and of G.C.E.O-level are to be taken as an indicator, the increasing popularity of biology is dramatic. From about 10 000 candidates in 1935, biology reached over 73 000 candidates in 1959. This compares with an increase for chemistry from about 27 000 in 1935 to about 59 000 in 1959 and for physics an increase from about 20 000 in 1935 to about 60 000 in 1959. That is to say, the demand for biology at O-level increased over the period by a factor of seven, compared with a doubling for chemistry and a tripling for physics over the same period. Again, biology is often advocated as a good subject for non-scientists to take in the sixth form (cf. Brierley 1960, pp. 85–102). Its 'cultural' aspects results from the fact that it deals with human beings among other creatures.

The approach of Nuffield biology is supposed to be that of the 'real biologist', in which a situation is described or suggested by means of testing an hypothesis about a situation. Only when apparatus is not available do pupils make use of second-hand data. The programme includes: Year I: introducing living things (naming things, cells, reproduction, insects, etc.); Year II: life and living processes (man and microbes, man against disease, movement, how plants reproduce and make seeds, man and his environment, etc.); Year III: the maintenance of life (how breathing takes place, obtaining energy, plants and the atmosphere, the uneven distribution of organisms, etc.); Year IV: Living things in action (habitat, cells, and water, mass-flow systems in plants, the behaviour of organisms, detecting changes in the environment, how man may affect his surroundings, etc.); Year V: The perpetuation of life (the similarities and differences in living things, how genes work, evolution, etc.).

Again, the method of teaching is essentially heuristic. Observations and experiments are the main part of the pupils' work and the questions posed in the pupils' texts can only be answered from the results of the experimental exercises. Throughout the programme emphasis is put on the collection of quantitative data, not as an end in itself but so that numeracy may be developed in the context of biology.

This brief discussion of the various subjects covered by the Nuffield programme may suggest that programmes of combined science have been neglected. This is not the case. A combined science section began in 1965, drawing on the materials developed in the O-level sections. In 1969, *Dialogue* (p. 12) discussing 'Science: Nuffield and the Schools Council', reported that

It is considered that unification of a wide range of subject matter can best be achieved by one teacher working in one laboratory with one class while the subject matter developed by combined science is grouped around ten topics: the world around us; looking for patterns; how living things began; air; electricity; water; small things; earth; insects; energy.

The programme of combined science was designed for the age-group 11–13; since 1969, a programme of integrated science has been developed for the 13–16 age-group.

These attempts to produce an integrated approach are very much in line with the recommendations of the Newsom Committee (Central Advisory Council for Education 1963), who noted (para. 423) that too much science teaching 'is of the nature of confirming foregone conclusions. It is a kind of anti-science, damaging to the lively mind, maybe, but deadly to the not so clever.' The Newsom Report emphasized the importance of relevance of science for the young school-leaver.

To examine the possibilities of integration, the Nuffield Foundation, which had been since 1961 developing science O-levels and science for the 8–13-year-olds (later 5–13-year-olds), commissioned five of Her Majesty's Inspectors to investigate and assess the situation and recommend what was needed. The resulting study was published as the Schools Council working paper No. 1, *Science for the young school leaver* (Schools Council 1965). This paper developed eight themes which, it was argued, would suit the Newsom ability range (Fig. 4.1).

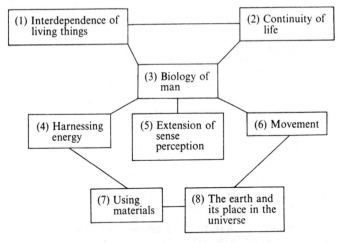

Fig. 4.1. The eight themes proposed in *Schools Working Paper* No. 1 for the young school-leaver (Schools Council 1965).

The Schools Council working paper stresses how it is important for the Newsom pupil that his science as a whole should have some significance of pattern and ultimately 'add up'. It quotes from the Newsom Report (para. 426): 'The field of science is so wide that what is done in schools can jump from one facet of the subject to another without much sense of cohesion developing.' The working paper emphasizes that the interest of the pupil is essentially of two kinds: an immediate intrinsic interest in the work in hand, and the broader interest of relevance to the modern scene. It must be made apparent to the pupils that the knowledge they are gaining, by whatever newly-devised method, has a real and current value to them.

The eight themes which the working paper established could be fully expounded or simply linked lightly with other fields or subjects. Although one volume was produced for each theme, these are merely for reference. There is a danger, which the Nuffield programme all along seeks to avoid, that teachers will plough through Nuffield as they would plough through any 'syllabus'. To adopt the 'covering-the-field' approach would be death to the Nuffield scheme as to any other scheme of science education.

By the end of 1969, over a million pounds had been spent by the Nuffield Foundation in their science curriculum development programme, probably the largest single investment in science education in the United Kingdom; but change is still relatively slow.

Reviewing the attitude of teachers to the introduction of Nuffield chemistry, Jenkins (1967) has commented that change is hampered by the fear of teachers hampering children in their examinations, and thus not daring to embark on new schemes. In a survey among teachers of chemistry, the biggest single reason he found for not 'going Nuffield' was that of the 'possible damaging effect' of a Nuffield O-level on pupils who might have to cope with an 'ordinary' A-level or a degree course. Thus do examinations stultify reform, not by their content (for many of the examination boards do all they can to develop curricula) but simply by the undue reverence they receive in a highly competitive educational system.

Curriculum reform has to take account of the context of the curriculum, who takes it, what influences them apart from the school, what else a course can build on. The Nuffield model of a development project consists of determining the objectives; producing materials and methods; conducting restricted trials; revising and evaluating the material; retraining teachers; and distributing materials. As Peter Kelly notes (1969, pp. 503–4) 'this system at first sight appears to be efficient but why, as far as one can tell, has the influence of all the development projects completed so far been clearly limited and the rate at which their influence has permeated educational institutions been invariably less than anticipated?' The focus of any curriculum is the student, and he stresses that it is with this in mind that efforts are being made to change the mechanisms which dictate the students' education.

At this point, a brief review of the main factors inhibiting curriculum change is appropriate.

4.4. The main factors inhibiting curriculum change in science

Some of the factors inhibiting curriculum change in science are simple, some are complex. At the risk of oversimplification, the principal factors involved seem to be the following.

(1) Certain organizational factors inhibit change. For example, the Schools Council is not always popular with teachers, being thought of as too theoretical and too distant from the teacher. This is not necessarily true, but schools in the United Kingdom are not used to any central control. The examining boards have been accepted as external forces which are at best necessary evils. Reform initiated from the *schools themselves* in C.S.E. and G.C.E. is an idea foreign to many teachers. Again, teachers' centres—set up to introduce teachers to new ideas—are new and unfamiliar, and teachers may not have the time or inclination to attend them.

(2) Science teachers, like other teachers, have come up through the old system. They managed the work and coped with the material, and often they do not see the need for reform.

(3) Many schools do not have enough equipment or space to go in for science in a big way. Large classes, against which teachers' organizations are vigorously campaigning, are an important inhibitor of curriculum change, especially in science. Nuffield science in particular, which requires classes of not more than thirty-two, is likely to suffer from the difficulty of exercising control in large classes.

(4) Science seems particularly susceptible to examinations pressure. There is a widespread mythology that a certain amount of 'ground' has to be 'covered'. Indeed, there is a measure of truth in this, for if some material does have to be covered for the examinations, it has to be covered *wholly* if pupils are to understand it. The arts have more freedom in this respect, for students can start the study of history, for example, at any point.

(5) An important factor is the current shortage of science teachers.

Many science teachers are grossly overworked and some are under-qualified in the subjects they are required to teach. There is a conflict of opinion about the B.Ed. degree (some say that it has become more specialized) but very few B.Ed. courses have any science in them unless they are specifically for science teachers, although there are some which aim particularly at integration (cf. Gill 1970, pp. 195–201). A survey among colleges of education carried out in 1968 showed that in those which specialized in science courses, only 520 out of 820 places could be filled (cf. Judge 1969, p. 428).

The shortages in the United Kingdom are for secondary school teachers as a whole, not just science teachers. The proportion of secondary school teachers, for example, coming out of college fell from 40 per cent of the total in 1963 to 22 per cent of the total in 1967. The Department of Education and Science reported (1969) that of teachers already in service, 90 per cent of the graduates were in secondary schools, and 70 per cent of these graduates had degrees in the arts. Of the science graduates, one-third were in mathematics, one-third in chemistry, and the rest were in physics and biology.

(6) The constitution of, and relationship between, the examining boards is another factor. Although in theory the C.S.E. and G.C.E. boards are all part of the same system and all link up with the Schools Council, the C.S.E. and G.C.E. boards rarely meet each other. Indeed, there is a certain degree of tension between them and a certain sense of competition, which seems strange if the boards are aiming at different sectors of the ability groups. If, as a result of the proposals for a common system of examining at 16-plus (Schools Council 1971), a single examination emerges, based upon the C.S.E. Mode III type of examination, this particular type of inhibition on curriculum change may disappear. Meanwhile, G.C.E. boards in particular are not constitutionally designed to permit new develop-ments to be examined promptly. As the secretary of one regional examining board said (in private correspondence) even the most in-terested teacher can scarcely be expected to wait three or four years between submitting his ideas and seeing his pupils examined in accordance with them.

(7) Although opportunities for bold experiments exist, particularly in C.S.E., teachers are often unwilling to take risks. Because C.S.E. is new, and has emphasized experiment, it runs the risk of being accused of being rough-and-ready. In some areas, papers have been produced which have stuck closely to Mode I examinations. G.C.E.

board secretaries have cited cases of C.S.E. papers which had more factual material in them than their counterpart G.C.E. papers, and were simply diluted G.C.E. Facts are easy to examine; initiative in experiment is difficult to examine. Hesitancy with the imaginative possibilities of Mode III is therefore to be expected.

(8) Another factor is that G.C.E. boards in particular are essentially 'in business'. Schools can in theory, and given time, choose their examining board for any or all subjects. If the school does change, a board may lose fees and thus income. Thus an examining board is hardly in a position to crash reform through without ensuring full or partial agreement from the schools which might take newly-formed examinations. This point must be made to be fair to the G.C.E. boards, which are often accused of being inhibitors of change.

There have been several instances of examinations brought in by the boards which have failed to attract schools, even though the examinations are clearly worked out and academically exciting. An A-level examination in modern history and contemporary society, for example, attracted only about 200 candidates at its inception; the number then fell away to 'a mere handful' in the words of the secretary of the examining board. The reluctance to accept new examinations can be explained by concern on the part of teachers that the subject will not be accepted by universities. The same board which introduced the modern history and contemporary society A-level introduced a unified science O-level which had very few candidates and is likely to be discontinued. As the secretary of one examining board put it, 'We find that most able and interested masters and mistresses in good schools are anxious to be progressive, but they are saddled with the necessity of trying to get G.C.E. passes for mediocre pupils. Sometimes it is this latter response which sways them rather than the former.'

(9) Acceptance by universities is another factor which makes curriculum change difficult especially in the G.C.E. Although there is now a Standing Conference on university entrance, communication between universities, G.C.E. examination boards, and schools is slow and cumbersome. Although, in theory, it is up to the schools to decide what to teach and then to ask the examining boards to provide the necessary examinations, it may well be that the universities do not fully appreciate the effect which their entrance requirements have on the entire system of secondary education, especially

in schools in which the G.C.E. is taken. Because of the vast prestige of university education—a prestige which is irrespective of the value of the particular subjects studied as preparation for work and living—attainment of a university place is the crowning achievement of much school education. Unless universities make vigorous attempts to encourage curriculum change, it is likely that the dead hand of the past will for many years determine the quality and types of curriculum change which can be brought about.

The professionalization and bureaucratization of science is responsible for the severe, specialized demarcation of 'subjects', and this demarcation into subjects percolates through the educational system down to O-level. The fate of science education for non-scientists, as will be shown in subsequent chapters, probably rests primarily with the universities, although the responsibility appears to be with the schools.

5 Science in Secondary Education: The Sixth Form

WHAT science is taught or could be taught to non-specialists at sixth-form level? In theory, before entering the sixth form all pupils are non-specialists, although the evidence cited from the Barnard and McCreath (1970) study suggests that the seeds of specialization are sown earlier. At sixth-form level, specialization has become overt.

The operational definition of a sixth-form pupil adopted here will be the one used in the survey *Sixth Form Pupils and Teachers* carried out by the Government Social Survey (now the Social Survey Division of the Office of Population Censuses and Surveys) in the late 1960s (Schools Council 1970); that is, a pupil in the sixth form (or equivalent) of secondary school or in his sixth or subsequent year of secondary school (or the equivalent year, if his secondary education started other than at the age of eleven). Although these pupils represent only 10·6 per cent of the age-group 16–18 (cf. p. 405 of the Schools Council survey), they are a particularly important sector of the age-group, and the problems of keeping them in touch with science culture may be clearly seen in the education with which they are provided.

In the Schools Council sixth-form survey, a sample of over 4000 pupils was interviewed in depth. The picture which emerges from the interviews is one of a sixth form dominated by the aspirations of its pupils to enter universities: 53 per cent of the pupils planned to take full-time university courses (63 per cent of boys and 38 per cent of girls). These pupils clearly had in mind the best way of satisfying university entrance requirements. However, the picture is complicated by the fact that more than 40 per cent of sixth-formers did not intend to apply for university entry: 14 per cent wished to attend colleges of education, 8 per cent chose other institutions offering full-time courses of higher education, and 17 per cent wished to go directly into employment—possibly employment with a component of in-service instruction (cf. p. 55 of the Survey).

The problem of providing a balanced education in the sixth form is clearly daunting. Apart from the diversity of pupils, there is the problem of maintaining cultural balance in view of the highly competitive nature of university entry, especially in the non-scientific fields. Universities require two passes at G.C.E. Advanced level for entry; and many departments in practice require three passes in related subjects. The majority of teachers, the Schools Council survey showed (para. 481) were on the whole satisfied with the A-level syllabus for their main teaching subject, although a third would have liked to see major changes; but teachers were by no means favourably disposed to the specialized *grouping* of A-level subjects into arts or science blocks. The survey showed (para. 333) that teachers by and large favour courses which require the study of some subjects in depth, but they attach equal importance to pupils having a wide general education in other subjects. Very few would advocate complete specialization in two or three subjects only. In recent years, there have been increasing demands from a variety of sources for a variety of reasons for a less specialized sixth-form curriculum.

One of the obvious causes for concern is that the excessive specialization in the sixth form, and indeed the specialization that exists at O-level constrains pupils to make irrevocable choices for arts- or science-based careers at a very early age. The Dainton Committee's *Enquiry into the flow of candidates in science and technology into higher education* (Council for Scientific Policy 1968) was particularly concerned with the factors affecting career choice in science and the possible damaging effects on the nation's activity in science and technology of able students being effectively cut off from science and technology by too early decisions. They recommended (para. 174) a broad span of studies in the sixth form, so that irreversible decisions for or against science, engineering, and technology might be postponed as late as possible. Indeed, the Dainton Committee specifically recommended (para. 178) that all pupils should study mathematics until they leave school, and only in exceptional circumstances should it be possible or desirable for a pupil to opt out. In this, they were concerned not only with students specializing in various science subjects but with pupils in all disciplines. Although the content of the curriculum was beyond the scope of their enquiry, they distinguished (para. 178, p. 89) some characteristics of mathematical achievement in relation to future demands of employment:

(i) Mathematics as a means of communicating quantifiable ideas and information.

(ii) Mathematics as a training for discipline of thought and for logical reasoning.

(iii) Mathematics as a tool in activities arising from the developing needs of engineering, technology, science, organisation, economics, sociology, etc.: the growth of numerical analysis and electronic computation is a powerful example.

(iv) Mathematics as a study itself, where development of new techniques and concepts can have economic consequences akin to those flowing from scientific research and development.

Although mathematics is being considered in this book only as an ancillary skill in science, the Dainton Committee's concern points to the principal range of problems with which the planners of the sixth-form curriculum are faced. Various possibilities have been proposed for mitigating the effects of over-specialization in the sixth form: for example, the mixing of A-levels, the modification of A-level examinations, the introduction of examined minority studies, or a combination of examined studies including general studies examined or otherwise. This chapter will examine the merits and defects of some of the principal schemes proposed.

5.1. The possibility of mixing G.C.E. A-levels

The principal attractions of achieving a balanced education (for non-specialists including some science) through a mixture of G.C.E. A-levels lie in three facts: (*a*) G.C.E. A-levels are public examinations which provide universities with reasonably comparable methods of measuring the attainments of different pupils from different schools, (*b*) the universities have it in their power to modify their entrance requirements for A-levels, and (*c*) the examining boards who set the A-level examinations can, in consultation with teachers through the various organizations which exist for this purpose, modify the syllabus and method of examining without much difficulty. As it happens, 72 per cent of sixth-formers at the time of the survey were taking three or more A-levels and a further 19 per cent were taking one or two A-levels (Schools Council 1970, p. 36). On the grounds that it is often prudent not to try to bring about too drastic a change at any one time, there would seem to be a strong case for attacking the problem of over-specialization through A-levels, which in terms of their content satisfy the majority of teachers; in terms of their 'currency' value are useful to universities; and are already part of the accepted, though as we shall see not often *willingly* accepted, way of life of sixth-formers.

One of the most vigorous proponents of an attack on the existing A-level system has been A. D. C. Peterson, Director of the Oxford University Department of Education, who pressed for a sixth-form curriculum of four advanced level G.C.E. subjects which between them would contain elements of scientific and non-scientific studies, and would cover the moral, aesthetic, logical, and empirical aspects of knowledge and understanding (Peterson 1960*a*). In an article attacking what he calls 'the myth of subject-mindedness' (Peterson 1960*b*, pp. 223–4) he notes that the maximum proportion of time spent by pupils at French lycées on science and maths has varied from 64 to 71 per cent, with the minimum time to be spent ranging from 26 to 35 per cent. Compared with this, Peterson noted that the English boy could spend a maximum of 75–90 per cent of his time on science and mathematics and a minimum of about 0–7 per cent. At the time of his survey Peterson noted the remarkably high proportion of pupils who, given a four-subject course, would have chosen a combination of arts and science subjects. This was 72 per cent in France, 69·1 per cent in Germany, and 57·5 per cent in England. In his article, Peterson (1960*b*, p. 231) concludes that specialism by 'sides' is forced on pupils by the system and by economic pressures. He argues that 'it is possible to be passionately interested in both physics and literature and it should be the aim of sixth-form education to encourage this rather that to prohibit it on the grounds that it does not conform to some artificially determined and narrowly limited "unity" '. He goes on to argue that 'The English curriculum is out of step; it compels too early a choice between arts and science; it provides no real general education; it starves either the moral and aesthetic or the logical and empirical development of our ablest adolescents; and no valid justification for it has been found.' To remedy the situation, Peterson proposes four A-levels of reduced factual content but spanning the traditional disciplines.

A similar proposal is contained in *A joint university–schools proposal for the revision of sixth form curricula and examinations,* a report of a working party set up by the university and schools committee of the University of Bristol (Bristol University 1968). The working party (see p. 7) rejected the suggestion that sixth-form studies should be based on a 'common core' of one or more compulsory subjects. They argued that it would be unfair for those who seem to be constitutionally innumerate to require them to pursue mathematics beyond an O-level course; and similar considerations apply to languages. It is inappropriate to use A-level English as a test of basic literacy; they argued that this should be tested at a lower level. They nevertheless hoped that more pupils would wish to continue with mathematics to A-level at the somewhat reduced level implied by a four-subject or five-subject A-level pattern.

The Bristol University working party were conscious of the fact that in either a four- or five-subject pattern the extent of possible choice would be limited by timetable and staffing difficulties, but they believed that the advantages of such a pattern outweigh the disadvantages. Whether a four- or a five-subject pattern is adopted, they propose that the subjects acceptable for university entrance should be divided into two or three groups, and that university aspirants should be required to take not more than three subjects from any one group. As a possible two-group pattern, they suggest:

Group I: maths G, maths M, physics, chemistry, physical science, botany, zoology, biology, geology, geography.

Group II: English, history, ancient history, languages, economics, politics, business studies, music art.

As possible three-group pattern they suggest:

Group I: maths G, maths M, physics, chemistry, botany, zoology, geology.

Group II: physical science, biology, geography, economics, politics, business studies, music, art.

Group III: English, history, ancient history, languages, divinity.

Maths M is intended to supplement Maths G for pupils wishing to read mathematics at the university; Maths G is intended to serve a much wider audience. Physical science would be a combined course in physics and chemistry, as in the Nuffield project; this subject could not be combined with physics or chemistry, and likewise biology could not be combined with botany or zoology.

Each subject would typically be studied for five or six periods per week, with a further five periods devoted to general studies and five or six periods for other activities. With either of the groupings proposed, it would be possible for pupils who have firmly decided on their vocation to achieve a reasonable degree of specialization, while those who are still uncertain whether to turn towards science or towards arts or social science would be able to keep their options open by a judicious choice of subjects. If the options are really to remain open, the working party argued, universities must be ready to accept on an equal footing those who have taken, say, only two science subjects and those who have taken three. They recommended that course requirements should as far as possible include only two named subjects.

A valuable refinement which the Bristol working party recommended is that of having 'A' and 'B' papers in each subject. Both 'A' and 'B' papers would be based on the same syllabus, but the 'A' paper would aim to test mainly achievement, and the 'B' paper mainly potential. 'A' papers should include a fairly large number of questions with little or no choice, to test the basic coverage of a suitably reduced and reformed syllabus. 'B' papers, on the other hand, could offer a wide choice of more demanding questions. The working party argued that the total examination load should be no more demanding than at present. The obvious implication for the universities is that if the time spent on each A-level subject were reduced from eight periods per week to five, university teaching would have to start at a lower level. The working party believed that many departments would nevertheless find it possible to retain a three-year degree course of much the same standard as at present, and some departments might even find it an advantage to have a broader base on which to build. In general, they argued, conceptual grasp of a subject is more important for university entrants than detailed factual knowledge, and the use of 'B' papers should help to achieve this.

Universities might resist the broader base of knowledge of their intake for reasons which will be outlined in the next chapter, but it is highly likely that a modification of A-level syllabuses along the lines proposed by the Bristol working party and the possibility of taking a mixture would be widely welcomed in the schools. At the time of the Schools Council survey, 31 per cent of pupils were taking sciences only in their A-levels, 36 per cent arts only, 9 per cent social sciences with or without arts, and 14 per cent mixed (science with arts and/or social science) (Schools Council 1970, p. 42). However, in the survey of attitudes, it was found (para. 192) that appreciable proportions of the A-level specialists (36 per cent of those taking only science A-levels and 29 per cent of those taking only arts) would have liked to be studying a mixture of arts and science subjects. The survey showed (pp. 163–4) that

the reason given most frequently by scientists for not taking the mixed course they would have liked was the fear of jeopardising their careers— they believed that mixed 'A' levels would make it harder to get accepted for the university places or jobs of their choice. Other reasons given by scientists were that the arrangement of subjects in the timetable made it difficult to take art subjects they would have liked, or that mixed courses were not encouraged by their school staff and they had been required to specialize in either arts or science lower down in the school.
Among arts pupils who would have preferred mixed courses, dis- couragement by the school from combining arts and sciences, together with timetable problems were the most commonly given reasons for not taking mixed courses. Mentioned more frequently by arts than science pupils was that they were not good at, or had never done any, subjects from the other discipline. Arts pupils much less often than scientists cited career disadvantages as deterring them from taking mixed courses.

The survey revealed that teachers, too, thought it important for sixth-form pupils to be able to take a mixture of arts and science subjects at A-level. Asked whether they thought that pupils should be able to take a mixture of arts and science subjects at A-level, 74 per cent of the teachers said 'yes' (77 per cent of arts teachers; 67 per cent of science teachers; 78 per cent of practical/expressive teachers) as against only 23 per cent who said 'no' (p. 350). The overwhelm- ingly dominant reason why teachers thought it important for pupils to be able to take a mixture of arts and science at A-level was that they felt it would give a broader outlook and a better-balanced, more well-rounded course (49 per cent of all teachers). The teachers who thought it *not* important for pupils to be able to take a mixture of arts and science subjects at A-level (just under a quarter of all teachers) were asked why they thought this, and the most frequently given reasons (by 11 per cent of all teachers) was that university entrance and careers requirements made mixed A-level courses impractical (p. 353).

It is clear that the desire which Peterson discovered for a wider

G

mix of subjects and for postponing crucial decisions about career choice still prevails, not only among pupils but also among teachers, and that Peterson's diagnosis of the cause for conservatism still holds, namely that pupils and their teachers are afraid of jeopardizing chances in the highly competitive university entrance race.

5.2. Specialization and supplementary courses

The second approach to the sixth-form curriculum is to accept the fact, and incidentally the value, of the high degree of specialization which universities seem to require. For example, Lord James (1949, pp. 672–7) has argued that there is no substitute for the intellectual and moral stimulus of grappling with really difficult ideas in a chosen subject. He argues that the performance of a piece of research, however humble, is not a narrowing but a broadening experience if we consider the personality of the student rather than his stock of information. He argues that it is unfortunately true that many criticisms of the high standards reached in sixth forms ignore this aspect of education as providing depth of experience. He comments (pp. 673–4):

A boy will trespass into first year university work, not because he is driven to do so in order to win a scholarship, but because he enjoys pushing on to prospects that he finds challenging and exciting. Great harm will be done to education in its broadest sense, if our approach to sixth-form studies is to find out what a boy likes doing and make sure that he does not do very much of it.

The principle of specialization received its chief accolade from the Crowther Committee's Report *15 to 18* (Central Advisory Council for Education 1959). The Committee stated (p. 261): 'We are agreed in accepting and endorsing the English principle of specialisation, or intensive study as it would be better described.' The Committee argued (paras. 387f.) that the ablest boys and girls are ready and eager by the time they are sixteen to get down to the serious study of some one aspect of human knowledge which, with the one-sided enthusiasm of the young, they allow for a time to obscure all other fields of endeavour. 'Subject-mindedness' they argue, is one of the marks of the sixth form. This supposition, as we have seen above, has been seriously questioned.

The second step in the Crowther Committee's argument is that as a pupil goes deeper and deeper in a subject he acquires self-confidence in his growing mastery of the subject. No longer does he rely on textbooks; no longer does he accumulate largely isolated pieces of information and separate, unrelated skills. He begins to assume responsibility for his own education.

The third step in the case for specialization is that, through this discipline, a pupil can be introduced into one or two areas which throw light on the achievement of man and the nature of the world he lives in.

The fourth step in the argument is that, given the right teaching, a pupil will by the end of his school days begin to come out on the further side of 'subject-mindedness'. (The Committee gave no evidence that this in fact occurs.)

The Crowther Committee criticized the idea of a mixture of A-levels on the grounds, first, that the coherence achieved by one subject continually reinforcing another so that teaching and learning may be enriched by cross-references, would be lost. Secondly, they objected that the essential qualities of a subject, as distinct from its particulars, would be likely to be overlooked in such a programme of study. The Committee singled out three elements of a sound sixth-form curriculum (para. 410):

> The first and largest should be the specialist element, on which a boy will spend, say, two-thirds of his time in school and much the greater part of his homework. Secondly there should be the common element, when scientists and arts specialists would come together. And thirdly, so to speak between the other two, there should be the complementary element, whose purposes—and in our view they must in the main be pursued separately—are to save the scientists from illiteracy and the arts specialists from innumeracy.

The Committee recommended that the minority-type science for the arts specialist should come from a specially tailored course. They objected to the idea of such special courses being examined by traditional examinations and recommended a form of internal assessment with outside moderation.

This policy recommendation of the Crowther Committee has been extensively discussed, and some proposals of suitable courses in science for arts specialists have been made to fit the minority time requirement (see Brierley in *Schools Council Working Paper* No. 4, 1966).

In their *Working Paper* No. 5, *Sixth form curriculum and*

examinations (1966), the Schools Council proposed a possible pattern of sixth-form studies which attempted not only to reconcile the Crowther affirmation of the principle of the study in depth with the Peterson plea for a wider range of examinable studies, but also to nurture the growth of general studies. Within the pattern proposed (pp. 12f.), major courses are envisaged as two-year courses, each occupying about eight weekly periods of 40 minutes; some of the eight would be devoted to teaching, some to private study. These courses would involve the study of a subject in depth similar to that now required for G.C.E. Advanced level and would also require about as much time as present G.C.E. courses. A minor course of the sort envisaged would be one absorbing about half as much time as a major course; it would spread over two years of sixth-form work using about four weekly periods including teaching and private study. Examinations set on these minor courses would be expected to assess work of a type and standard to be expected from pupils more mature than those for whom G.C.E. O-level examinations are designed. The working paper proclaimed that various educational needs can be identified which it might be possible to meet with appropriately designed minor courses of advanced study:

(a) It might be possible to devise a minor course which would 'support' or be ancillary to a major course. Thus a pupil 'majoring' in two foreign languages might take a supporting minor course in history.

(b) A minor course might be chosen by a pupil as offering a contrast to his major studies. Thus a pupil 'majoring' in science might wish to take a minor course in a foreign language.

(c) There will undoubtedly be some pupils whose abilities and interests would best be served by a broad, well-balanced curriculum, rather than a highly specialised one. Minor courses might well comprise the main ingredients of the curriculum of such pupils who would not wish to follow a major course or, perhaps, not more than one. Such pupils, too, might well be able to afford more time for the minor courses they take than would pupils who take two major courses.

The Crowther Committee's recommendation of a common course for all the sixth form to supplement the specialist studies and the complementary studies, would be met by the provision of general studies, of which more will be said below. University selection in the scheme proposed in *Working Paper* No. 5 would be supplied by the examination of two major courses and two minor courses, one at least of which would be of a contrasting character.

Not only did *Working Paper* No. 5 examine the policy questions at issue, but its Appendix B, 'The curricula possibilities of a pattern of sixth-form work based on major courses, minor courses and general studies' provided model timetable plans, consisting of various blocks of major and minor studies, which would facilitate a suitable combination of studies. But in spite of the thoroughness with which these models were prepared, the scheme was subjected to severe criticism, much of which is contained in *Working Paper* No. 16, *Some further proposals for sixth-form work* (Schools Council 1967). Typical criticisms include the following (p. 3):

(a) The introduction of minor courses in all or almost all of the subjects in which major courses are provided would undoubtedly tend to reduce the total number of such subjects which could be retained in the curriculum. It is apparent that schools regard the possibility of such a sacrifice with concern.

(b) While in large sixth forms it might prove feasible to introduce a satisfactory range of minor courses, including alternative minor courses in the same subject, the possibility of doing this would be very much less in smaller sixth forms, and in some cases because of staffing limitations it might be difficult to provide a minor course in some subjects at all. There is general concern that any new curricula patterns should not favour the large sixth form against the small any more than at present.

(c) Many schools will be able to offer single minor courses only and it is doubtful whether one and the same minor course designed to be externally examined can serve the needs of pupils coming into it with varying levels of educational achievement and with different reasons in mind for taking it.

(d) There is also a strong feeling that the limitation of the influence of external examining to two-thirds of the sixth formers work does not go far enough. The implication here is not that the proportion of intellectually demanding work in a pupil's time-table should be reduced, but that some of it should be assessed otherwise than by formal external examination.

(e) It has also been stressed by some critics of working paper No. 5 that the reduction to two major courses imposes a limitation on the pupil's subsequent choice of university course or career, or to put it another way, imposes an undesirably early choice, namely at the stage of entry to the sixth form.

High among the priorities in the further proposals for sixth-form work was that of providing a pattern of sixth-form studies which met the respective needs of different types of pupil in the sixth form :

for example, students taking two, three, or four A-level subjects, but no O-level subjects; A-level students taking or repeating individual O-level subjects, mainly but not exclusively in the first year of the sixth form; first-year sixth-form O-level candidates studying for A-level in a single subject; first-year sixth-form O-level candidates, some of them first takers, some repeaters, some both; other pupils with different external examination objectives or none at all. All these categories exist, and as the sixth-form survey (Schools Council 1970) has shown, over 40 per cent of sixth-formers are not aiming at university entry. It is therefore inappropriate to devise a syllabus which is designed solely for university entry.

Working Paper No. 16 reiterates the principle that the curriculum of every candidate for university entrance should include two A-level subjects, broadly as at present understood. In addition, the paper suggests that each school should place on offer a range of *elective courses*. These elective courses would be structured ones reflecting the teaching power available and the needs and interests of pupils in any particular school. The individual pupil's choice of elective courses could be such that they support or complement the remainder of his sixth-form work, to give a spread of subjects. Like the minor courses proposed in *Working Paper* No. 5, each elective course might be thought of as occupying four periods a week, including one of private study, for one year. Some of the electives could become 'double' subjects by extending over two years, possibly in successive parts capable of separate assessment.

Central to the idea of elective courses is that of the freedom of the school to devise its own syllabus. External advice on the construction of suitable syllabuses and moderation in the assessment of them would not only help the schools to state the aims and content of their syllabuses but would also make it clear to the universities what might be expected of candidates who had followed those syllabuses. The proposed elective courses could then, of course, be taken by any of the different categories of sixth-form pupil, from those taking A-levels to those finishing some O-levels in the sixth form and wishing to take some course which extended them beyond O-level.

However, in spite of the clarity and confidence with which these new proposals for electives are put forward by the Schools Council Working Party, there is nevertheless a note of anxiety about the possible reaction of universities to this. For example (para. 19):

How can pupils be sure that they are not being handicapped by only doing two 'A' levels? Would it be sufficient for all universities to affirm as a convention of selection that as from a certain date they would take no account of any more than two? And perhaps, as a corollary, that they would regard as a negative factor any deficiency in the number of electives or in school evidence about general studies? Could the universities give sufficient assurance to schools that such a policy would in practice be reflected in the decisions of individual faculties or subject departments with the actual responsibility for selection? If there is doubt about the answers to these questions, would it be necessary, desirable or practicable to eliminate the uncertainty by adding to the regulations governing the conduct of the examinations one which made it impossible for more than two 'A' levels to be taken, say, in any one year? These are tough questions, but they must be answered in ways which satisfy pupils (and their advisers) that changes in the sixth form curriculum, however beneficial they may be educationally, will not in any way change their personal prospects of advancing to higher education.

Indeed, in the highly competitive situation of university entry, it is difficult to see which school would be first in risking the chances of its pupils by undertaking such a pattern of sixth-form studies.

5.3. A modified examinations structure

A third approach to the problem of achieving a more balanced curriculum in sixth-form education was embodied in a joint statement by the Standing Conference on University Entrance and the Schools Council Joint Working Party on Sixth Form Curriculum and Examinations (SCUE and Schools Council 1969). The possibility of a mixture of A-level subjects, as discussed above, would necessarily involve an alteration to the content of A-levels. Again, the elective courses proposed in the Schools Council *Working Paper* No. 16 also introduced the idea of a different type of course. However, the central feature of the joint statement was to propose a radically new structure of examinations for the sixth form.

The objectives of the joint statement (SCUE 1969, p. 1) were wholly commendable:

We are agreed that our first aim is to identify the ways in which all sixth formers can receive a balanced education suited to their needs as young people of 17 and 18 years of age. Their curriculum must not take its shape from external pressures exerted in the interests of some narrow view of what they may become; rather, it must grow from an understanding of what they are and need as sixth formers who will shortly be facing all the complex problems of living in the modern world.

Our second aim seems to us to be compatible with and to support the first. It is to enable young people to avoid commitments which unduly limit their choice of career or higher education.

The joint proposal was also concerned to provide for sixth-formers who have a variety of educational objectives. The most basic proposal was one for a new examination and a new general entry qualification for higher education. This examination was conceived of as a minimum general entry qualification for all sectors of higher education. It should be obtainable after a minimum of one year's study beyond C.S.E. or O-level. This general entry qualification was envisaged as a broad course of studies at a level about midway between the present ordinary level and advanced level.

The proposal was that the curriculum for at least the first year of sixth-form work would comprise the study of *five subjects* for about five-sevenths of the 35-period week. The remaining two-sevenths of the week would be devoted to unexamined studies and other activities. The basic objective of keeping options open as long as possible would be met only if the five subjects studied were spread over a reasonable spectrum of knowledge. General rules would have to be adopted to ensure that all pupils study some arts subjects and some scientific or mathematical subjects, while at the same time providing a fair measure of choice. This new examination was to be known as the *Qualifying Examination*. The joint proposals, in the third section of its annex, outlined a single grouping scheme which would need to be nationally agreed defining the groups of subjects from which students sitting the Qualifying Examination would have to select their five.

The joint proposal envisaged that the Qualifying Examination would have several uses (see pp. 4–5). Many pupils would take the examination in the full number of subjects at the end of one year in the sixth form; their results would be available when they applied for university and other places of full-time higher education, and would be of great value to selectors at an early stage in their work. The joint proposal did not expect universities to make places available solely on the basis of the Qualifying Examination but its use at the initial selection stage would, it was suggested, be much better than present practices, which sometimes use O-level results for this purpose.

To supplement the Qualifying Examination (or Q-level), the proposal suggested the provision of a higher-level examination to be taken at the end of the seventh year; this was to be called the *Further Examination* (or F-level). It was recommended that for those seeking university entrance or entry to other forms of higher education not more than three subjects would be required at this level and that of these as few as possible should be specified by name. The Further Examination was to be a single-subject, graded examination. Syllabuses would be designed to be of the standard corresponding to one year's work beyond the Qualifying Examination and the study of three subjects would occupy no more than five-sevenths of the working week; the remaining time would be devoted to unexamined studies and other activities. Like previous statements about the sixth-form curriculum, the joint proposal regarded general studies as a valuable part of the final years of sixth-form work.

The joint proposal recommended the universal introduction of the new examinations and suggested a schedule of possible activity for introducing them. In particular, the proposal pointed out that if the new pattern were not adopted universally but instead were made available as an alternative to the present system, then a situation would be created in which there were five major public examinations: C.S.E., G.C.E. O-level, G.C.E. Advanced level, the Qualifying Examination, and the Further Examination; the examination resources of the country might not be strong enough to bear such a load.

While the general objectives of the joint proposal are to be commended, there is a great deal to be criticized in the detail. From a purely academic point of view, there was a faint suggestion that by taking the Qualifying Examination after the first year in the sixth form the pupil would be getting over his general education requirements much as a child gets over measles early in life.

Secondly, it was not clear whether the G.C.E. O-level would disappear or not. At present, as has been pointed out above, C.S.E. is rapidly gaining popularity as a measure of achievement for the vast majority of pupils who leave secondary school before entering the sixth form and who do not have the academic potential or the particular desire to take G.C.E. O-level, which is overtly an academic examination aimed at the top 20 per cent of the age-group in terms of ability. If G.C.E. O-level were not abolished, the situation envisaged by the joint proposal would almost certainly come about;

that is to say, the sixth-former would take a public examination in each of three successive years. As Sir Desmond Lee (1970) has pointed out, examinations are never 'taken in one's stride' and Q-level would be a distraction to those seeking to settle down to serious study in the sixth form.

Thirdly, if universities and other institutions of higher education were serious about adopting the wide spread of examinations at Q-level as a *necessary* as well as sufficient minimum entrance requirement, and refused to take a student who failed to achieve a satisfactory standard within a stated group of subjects, awkward situations would have been likely to arise—as used to arise with the use of the English paper—and a student of undoubted brilliance in one subject might have been technically denied entrance to the institution of his choice through failure to meet the minimum entrance requirement.

There were of course many other academic and administrative objections to this proposal, but the main objection was that the proposed modified examinations structure would in itself have done nothing to mitigate the effects of overspecialized teaching; the power of universities to dictate, through their entry requirements, what is *actually* studied would in no way have been altered, and F-level would simply have taken over from A-level.

Most of the supposed benefits of Q-level (as a preliminary university guide for selection other than O-level) could very well be achieved by one of the ideas proposed by the University and Schools Committee of the University of Bristol (Bristol University 1968). They suggest (p. 12, para. 11) the possibility of an internal part I examination at the end of the first year in the sixth form. Such an examination need not be a great deal more forbidding than the ordinary school examination which pupils would otherwise take. If the results of such examinations, and possibly even papers or dissertations written by pupils, were to be available to university selectors, they would probably take much less account of O-levels in making their preliminary selection.

5.4. 'General studies' science in the sixth form

Although it is prodigiously difficult to say exactly what is meant by the phrase 'general studies', all the proposals for curriculum reform in the sixth form recommend that some time be set aside for such studies. The sixth-form survey (Schools Council 1970, pp.

176–7) found that 67 per cent of sixth-form pupils said that they were taking general studies or discussion lesson courses. Indeed, there is a vigorous movement designed to strengthen this element of sixth-form work. The Schools Council have set up a special general studies project at the University of York, and two associations, the Association for Liberal Education and the General Studies Association, are dedicated to furthering the aims of general studies.

The principal aims of general studies have been conveniently summarized in the Schools Council *Working Paper* No. 25 *General Studies 16–18* (Schools Council 1969c, p. 8) as follows: First that general studies should help to mitigate the effects of specialization and give students a glimpse of achievement in spheres of knowledge other than those studied for A-level; secondly, to offer some education of the emotions through such subjects as music and art; thirdly, to show students the wider implications of their specialist subjects; fourthly, to give them an awareness of their place in society; and fifthly, to engender a capacity for making independent and critical judgements.

The methods by which teachers seek to achieve these aims are very diverse. However, *General Studies 16–18* (p. 9) again usefully categorizes four main approaches:

(a) Most common are courses based on familiar disciplines, sometimes extending them on to unfamiliar ground, e.g. contemporary world history, engineering, history of science, foreign literature, human biology, and evolution.

(b) Drama, creative work in the art room, music, home economics, film-making, woodwork, and metalwork form common parts of general studies courses which contrast with 'A' level work.

(c) Elements of unfamiliar disciplines, e.g. sociology, psychology, philosophy, anthropology, linguistics, cosmology, ethology.

(d) Planned inter-disciplinary studies, drawing upon either familiar or unfamiliar disciplines or on both, e.g. war and society, the history of Western civilization, society and the modern world, education, crime and law, cities, world poverty, religion.

One of the characteristic features of general studies is that they are frequently an unrelated addition to the timetable, not an integral part of it achieved by planning and co-ordination. It is deceptively easy to stretch the phrase 'general studies' to include all the varied non-A-level courses and activities in the sixth form, thereby destroying what is in fact a useful concept.

In seeking to define the essential characteristics of general studies, *Working Paper* No. 25 (Schools Council 1969c) identifies three central features. First, general studies courses are about things that matter; they deal with questions of common concern to students regardless of their disciplines. Secondly, they seek to explore general connections between what might otherwise appear to be isolated elements of knowledge. As the working paper puts it (p. 14): 'the facts, problems, ideas, events, or whatever is being studied have interesting inter-connections and repercussions, which teacher and students pursue without the guilty feeling of having "digressed" from a prescribed syllabus'. General studies frequently provide the opportunity for teachers to move outside academically defined disciplines and explore matters of common social concern with whatever skill and knowledge seems most suitable. Thirdly, there is emphasis in general studies upon the transfer of knowledge, skills, sensitivities, interests, and values. In this context, the word 'general' suggests that what students learn should be in the nature of skills which can be applicable in unforeseen situations: a command of written and spoken English; habits of careful observation, logical thought, systematic approach to problems encountered; critical questioning of accepted attitudes, and so on. Although these items are clearly features of the educational intention of traditional sub-jects, general studies are likely to be less concerned with the content of a particular subject than with the method of approach.

The overall objectives of general education are very highly rated by both pupils and teachers, according to the Schools Council sixth-form survey. When sixth-form pupils were questioned about general education, items highly favoured were: 'Offer you a wide selection of subjects from which to choose' (rated as extremely important by 72 per cent of sixth-form pupils), 'encourage you to read widely and follow your own interests in your reading' (54 per cent), 'ensure that you are aware of aspects of the subjects beyond those in the exam-ination syllabus' (49 per cent), and 'enable you to develop an interest in subjects other than those studied for examinations' (43 per cent) (Schools Council 1970, pp. 123–5). More pupils attached great im-portance to broadening education, as described by these items, than to having opportunities to study a subject in great depth.

Teachers showed a similar interest in general studies as a valuable part of the sixth-form curriculum (Schools Council 1970, pp. 357f.). Asked whether they considered general studies valuable for all sixth-formers, 84 per cent of the teachers interviewed (in a sample of over 1000) said 'yes' and only 5 per cent said 'no'. Again, 68 per cent of teachers thought that general studies were valuable for broadening the mind and providing a background to other studies. The small group of teachers (5 per cent) who did not think general studies a valuable part of the sixth-form curriculum said that there were organizational problems in providing general studies, such as a shortage of teachers, timetabling difficulties, and the need to divide pupils into small groups for them (p. 360). When one examines the part played by science in the general studies of students studying arts A-levels, the picture is rather disappointing; only 27 per cent of the arts specialists taking three A-levels also took some natural science in their general or non-examination courses (p. 182). Again, whereas 44 per cent of those taking three or more A-levels specializing in science were taking arts or social science subjects *for an examination*, only 12 per cent of arts A-level specialists were taking any sciences (p. 189). Perhaps this low figure is a reflection of teachers' ideas about what constitutes a satisfactory general education. Sixth-form teachers were asked how valuable they thought it was for all sixth-form pupils to do some English, some mathematics, and some science: 71 per cent said that it was very valuable for all to do some English, 18 per cent mathematics, and 19 per cent science (p. 382).

If science is indeed to become part of the general culture, and if sixth forms are one of the principal agencies through which culture is transmitted, it would seem highly desirable that science should feature more largely in sixth-form general studies than it does at present, whether or not pupils eventually take mixtures of A-levels or any other form of sixth-form curriculum. What objectives have been proposed for general studies science in the sixth form and what types of courses do teachers favour?

In *Science in sixth-form general education*, the Association for Science Education (1963) stated firmly that not only should all pupils follow a balanced course of science subjects up to the end of their fifth-form year, but that science should be studied by *all* pupils in the sixth form. The Association suggested a broad course designed to enable the pupils to attain greater general scientific literacy, not the specialist courses leading to A-level examinations. Unlike the Crowther Committee (who recommended special complementary studies in science for arts specialists), the Association emphasized that the further course of general study science is intended for all pupils and is *not* 'science for arts sixths'. Science specialists need it too, the Association argued, to supplement their specialist work in just a few branches of science; ideally, they argued, classes should contain both science and arts specialists, so that there is a representative cross-section of all specialist interests. The Association recognized that the majority of schools will probably not be able to provide more than two teaching periods a week for two years to the science work of the general studies course, but they suggest that this should be a minimum and that there should be further time available for private reading and essay-writing. (In fact, most schools set aside approximately seven periods a week out of thirty-five for non-examination and general studies subjects.) The Association bases its recommendation of courses upon this allocation of time. Compulsory examinations are not favoured, but questions set in general studies papers are. The science in sixth-form general education would be based upon a series of themes which the Association lists with reading matter and study suggestions. The themes include such topics as the nature of scientific thought, cosmology, energy, matter, life, behaviour, environment, and science and society.

Four studies have sought to discover what objectives science teachers thought most important in general education in the sixth form and to discover what kinds of courses are currently offered. Casey (1968, chapter II) describes how teachers in over 200 schools who replied to questionnaires rated a series of objectives which they considered to be important in sixth-form general education. In the affective domain, the objective 'to begin to understand the impact and implications of modern scientific achievements upon himself and society' received the highest rating (p. 260). The development of 'an enquiring and critical turn of mind' and the cultivation of an 'interest in the patterns and problems of scientific developments' were also extremely well received. Even the least favoured of affective objectives (an appreciation of the value of experimental work) was placed among the most popular one-third of objectives by both men and women. Also highly rated was 'the ability to evaluate conclusions in the light of the facts, observations, and experimental procedures on which they are based' (p. 284) and 'knowledge of the scientific approach to the study of phenomena', and also 'awareness about the extent of science's competence and limitations' reached the status of 'very important' in the men's ratings and only slighly lower in the women's ratings.

In another study Oliver and Lewis (1970) prepared a schedule of 120 topics, 40 from the arts, 40 from the social studies, and 40 from the scientific fields. The topics were rated for their importance as part of a sixth-form course in general studies by 36 university and college of education teachers in the Manchester area. Respondents were required to rate the items on a 9-point scale. All the teachers rated the following science subjects highly: science and everyday life, scientific concepts, and scientific methods; low ratings were given to such subjects as geology, meteorology, radio-astronomy, relitivity, and the physics of radio and television (p. 171). From the whole range of subjects, not simply the science subjects, the following topics were accorded a high rating by all the respondents. These topics indicate a range of general studies regarded as important in a sixth-form course.

(i) Cultivation of aesthetic values—with such topics as appreciation of art and appreciation of music.

(ii) Concern with religion and morals—with such topics as ethics, human rights, religion and life today, and comparative religion.

(iii) Development of mental skills—with such topics as clear thinking and creative writing.

(iv) Studies of current affairs—with numerous, wide-ranging and related topics such as current affairs, the social implications of science, social problems, economic problems of Britain today, and population problems.

(v) Aspects of science—with such topics as scientific concepts, scientific methods, science and everyday life, and social psychology.

Oliver and Lewis noted that sixth-form general studies are frequently planned over five terms, i.e., for two school years minus the final examination term, and many schools teach about ten topics in these five terms. Topics could, then, be selected from all the above categories and some schools, they suggested, might decide on two topics from each category. Oliver and Lewis did not attempt to prescribe any particular or uniform practice, but they noted that the opinions reported in their paper point to the existence of a moderately strong consensus among teachers in higher education about what general studies in the sixth form should include.

J. R. Baker (1969, pp. 176–83) of the School of Education, Leicester University, analysed information received from 254

Science in secondary education:

teachers who responded to a questionnaire. Although this number represents only 30 per cent of the total number of teachers approached, the replies indicate what kinds of science enthusiasts feel should be taught in sixth-form general studies. In terms of the type of course to be taught, the percentage of total mentions for various courses was as shown in Table 5.1.

TABLE 5.1.

Total mentions for sixth-form general studies (Baker 1969)

	(%)		(%)
Survey of science	15	Projects	13
Recent discoveries	6	Methods of science	12
Basic science	2	Philosophy of science	13
Depth study	4	History of science	16
Science and [topic unspecified]	8	Science in everyday life	3
Bridge study	4	Others	4

In terms of topics to be taught, respondents tended to suggest topics within their own areas of expertise more than topics from other sciences. The biologists, Baker noted, tended to suggest more topics than physicists or chemists, and genetics, evolution, and social biology easily top the list of topics suggested because of massive support from the biologists. Following these topics come energy, nuclear physics, technology, history, philosophy and methods of science, and synthetic materials. Among the various aims of the courses which were mentioned, the importance of cultivating an appreciation of science and scientists and an understanding of the effects of science on society stand out.

These attitudes to the aims of science in sixth-form education and to the methods of achieving them correspond very closely to practice as described in an earlier publication by Baker (1967). In a survey of 38 schools with well-developed general studies courses, he made the following rough classification of types of courses and frequency of occurrence:

History of science courses	16 schools
Survey of science courses	8 schools
Basic principles of science courses	8 schools
Methods of science courses	7 schools
Science ... and various topics	6 schools
Philosophy of science courses	4 schools

Depth studies	3 schools
Project work	1 school
O-level course	1 school
Practical course	1 school

In a later survey, Baker (1970) received information from 75 per cent of a stratified random sample of 300 schools which had sixth forms. From his information he noted (p. 27) that more than 40 per cent of arts sixth forms in all schools were not offered general studies science, that not more than 35 per cent had to do any general studies science and that for all those who have to do some general studies science, the average time spent on it is about one period per week.

Replies to a question on the types of course offered produced a pattern of activity similar to that shown in the earlier survey (Baker 1970, p. 31).

Survey of science today	39 schools
History of science	38 schools
Recent discoveries and future expectations	34 schools
Methods of science	25 schools
O-level science, e.g. human biology	21 schools
Philosophy of science	22 schools
Basic facts and principles of science	18 schools
Depth studies	15 schools
Science and ... [e.g. society]	14 schools
Projects	13 schools

As Baker notes, statements of the aims of general studies science necessarily vary in their shades of meaning, but the following were the most frequently mentioned.

Grasp of science for its effects on society	25 schools
Knowledge about science and scientists	16 schools
Interest outside specialization	15 schools
To keep arts side scientifically literate to reduce arts–science gulf	13 schools

In reviewing (in Chapter 2) the general objectives of science education for non-specialists and the specific objectives by which the general objectives could be met, stress was placed on the desirability of a student being characterized by a value or value complex—in science, for example, the willingness to revise judgements in the light of evidence. In the discussion of cognitive objectives, stress was put

H

on that of evaluation and the broadening of the foundation on which judgements were made. Again in discussing in Chapter 2 the methods by which science may be taught to non-scientists, the value of practical activity was emphasized. It is disappointing to note the relatively small amount of science featuring in sixth-form general studies courses for students taking arts A-levels and what appears to be a tendency to teach *about* science rather than to teach science.

This is not to say that the conventional science of the G.C.E. A-level need necessarily be taught. There is a good case for some general studies science which is new both to those taking arts A-levels and to those taking science A-levels; joint activity on the same piece of work might go some way to bridging what could otherwise be a gulf between the two types of learning. Newbold (1969, pp. 136–7), for example, suggests that the elements of literacy and numeracy in sixth-form education should appear in the common rather than the complementary section of that education. If it is accepted, he argues, that all sixth-form students should gain the all-round appreciation of values which these wider concepts imply, it is questionable if the sixth form should be further split in the process of acquiring them. He suggests that it is only by working together that sixth-form pupils will really get some measure of the depths of the studies followed and attitudes adopted by their fellow students, and at the same time achieve common ground with them.

This is not to say that there is no place in the curriculum for (say) arts students to follow a course in science on particular topics which the scientists have covered in their specialist work and with which they should be familiar (e.g. radio activity). But before such a course is provided, it should certainly be questioned whether its real value to the non-scientist is anything more than encyclopaedic knowledge; whether it is anything more than a superficial extension of already familiar 'O' level work; whether the course would in fact be of value to scientists also in that it would allow them to look at one of their own specialities from a different standpoint; whether this might not in any case be an opportunity for scientists to attempt to explain their own point of view to non-specialists; whether the possible advantages of further division of non-scientists from scientists outweigh the disadvantage of emphasising further the obvious differences between them. When a science for non-scientists (only) course is looked at in this way, it may be that its true worth will become apparent: perhaps only the occasional short course of this type will remain in the curriculum.

There is obviously opportunity for the undertaking by mixed groups of arts and science pupils of projects of social relevance with some scientific content.

But should these general studies in sixth-form science be examined? The Schools Council sixth-form survey (1970) asked teachers whether or not they were in favour of general studies being examined. On this issue (p. 361) 71 per cent of teachers were, in principle, against their being examined and only 16 per cent were completely in favour; 11 per cent saw some points in favour but others against. This might appear to be an overwhelming reason for abandoning the idea.

However, general studies are in fact already being examined. At least two examining boards offer a G.C.E. A-level in general studies, and the Schools Council sixth-form survey revealed (p. 38) that such A-levels were being taken and particularly by those who were preparing three, or in a few cases four, other subjects for A-level. Of those taking a total of four or more A-level subjects, 58 per cent were taking general studies, but only 2 per cent of those taking three A-levels were doing so and only 1 per cent of those taking one or two A-levels.

This relatively low proportion of students taking the A-level may be a reflection of the fact that it is not offered by all the boards. Where it is offered, it is extremely popular. The Northern Universities Joint Matriculation Board offers a general studies A-level which has been growing in popularity. In 1959 it was taken by 1530 candidates; in 1969 it was taken by 14 000 candidates (J.M.B. Statistics 1969, table 10). The J.M.B. general studies A-level now ranks second only to English in popularity.

Oliver (1961) has described the genesis of the examination and analysed the marking of it. In a later article (1965) he discussed the history and philosophy of science in the Joint Matriculation Board general studies examination. Some of the questions quoted in both these publications merit the charge that they test memorized pieces of information, and that the general studies paper is really only a collection of specific studies welded together. However, Oliver gives examples of some questions which would genuinely test the ability to evaluate a problem in scientific terms and the extent to which an individual is characterized by the values of a scientist. These could be answered without any prior knowledge of the subject-matter in hand. For example (Oliver 1961, p. 15):

8. Design an investigation to test *one* of the following hypotheses:

(a) that 'broken homes' contribute to delinquency.
(b) that the weather changes at the new moon.
(c) that learning ten lines of English poetry by heart each day for a month improves the memory for French vocabulary.
(d) that no prediction can be made, when children enter a Secondary School, about the likelihood of their passing in five subjects of the General Certificate of Education at the ordinary level.
(e) that detergent 'Sparko' cleans greasy dishes more effectively than detergent 'Spume'.

Consider such points as the data you would use or the observations you would make, and the reasoning by which you could reach a conclusion.

12. Scientific investigation is sometimes supposed to consist of 'experiments'. What is an experiment? By what means besides experiments is scientific enquiry conducted? Refer to examples.
13. Each of the following may be described as a scientist: An archaeologist, an astronomer, a botanist, a physicist, a psychologist. What have they in common?
14. Describe some scientific problem which has not yet been completely solved. How did it arise, what progress has been made towards solving it, and what difficulties still impede its solution?

Or again, a question from the 1963 examination (quoted in Oliver 1965, p. 31):

13. Design an investigation of *one* of the following problems, making clear the purpose of each step you suggest. Discuss the merits and weaknesses of your design.

(a) Does a dog distinguish between the colours blue and yellow?
(b) Does the use of a certain fertilizer by a farmer improve his crop of wheat?
(c) How well can one predict from G.C.E. marks in a certain subject which candidates would gain a degree if they followed a certain university course?

If the general transfer of skill which general studies seeks to achieve has in fact occurred, a pupil in the sixth form having undertaken *some* general studies science should be able to tackle these questions.

The advantages of A-levels as uniform measures of academic capability have been stressed earlier in this chapter. They commend themselves to universities as a uniform measure of excellence;

their content and method of examining can be altered with relative ease by the examining boards in consultation with the schools; they have the confidence of the pupils (even if they are disliked by them); and above all, are the most readily manipulable part of the curriculum. Three broad possibilities for achieving a better balanced sixth-form education, and in particular in maintaining a science component in the education of students majoring in the arts, present themselves.

First, a mixture of modified A-levels as recommended in the report by Bristol University (1968).

Secondly, general questions in existing A-levels requiring knowledge of other types of material than that traditionally covered by the subject. This type of question might meet with resistance by teachers and by pupils and would very likely be overlooked in favour of the 'safe' questions of the traditional sort.

Thirdly, a general studies A-level which requires pupils to answer questions from each of several sections representing arts, social sciences, and humanities. Such an A-level could even contain a mathematical component (associated with the science component or otherwise) which would provide an incentive to pupils to maintain their mathematical studies in the sixth form without the formality of a special elective subject or a special A-level. The general studies A-level would, therefore, seem to be in present circumstances the 'best buy'. Indeed, it has been claimed by Newbold (1969, p. 160) that:

There is an advance in 'scientific understanding' gained by non-scientist sixth form students in schools associated with the 'A' level examination in general studies, and that, overall, this is not matched by the other systems investigated. This is not to say that the 'understanding of science and its contribution to the intellectual, spiritual and physical aspects of our lives' cannot be achieved by other means—perhaps the gradual emergence of Nuffield science is a possibility here—but that 'A' level courses in general studies provide an established starting-point for the development of antidotes, in science at least, to the problems of sixth form over-specialisation.

6 Science for Non-Specialists at Universities

THE last chapter described how university entrance requirements restrict experiment in the combination of courses of G.C.E. Advanced level and in the fabrication of new courses. Liberalization of university entrance requirements would almost certainly be a spur to curriculum change in the schools and, consequently, to the inclusion of some science in the education of non-scientists. If reform in this area is the prerogative of the universities, it might seem that universities would be the places in which the most imaginative experiments in science education for non-specialists would take place for, in principle, universities can teach and examine whatever they wish to. Yet science courses for non-specialists are still comparatively rare at British universities. This chapter examines the reasons for this state of affairs and discusses the types of courses offered and the constraints operating on those who provide them.

Since the Second World War, there has been widespread advocacy of the virtues of general education. In the United States of America, for example, an interdisciplinary committee of faculty members at Harvard University produced in 1945 *General education in a free society*, a book which influenced not only the curriculum of Harvard itself but the curricula of other universities in America. A similar debate at Washington University resulted in *The purposes of higher education*, a thorough discussion edited by Huston Smith (1955). Daniel Bell's *The reforming of general education* (1966) reviews the discussion which took place at Columbia University.

Similar discussion has taken place in the United Kingdom. A succession of high-powered committees has urged universities to pay greater attention to general education. In their development report for the quinquennium 1952–7, the University Grants Committee (1958) urged that students be given information which should be both wide and deep. Noting that the acquisition of specialized knowledge is not the only, or the most important, benefit which a student should derive from his course, and emphasizing that the first duty of the university was to teach the student how to think, the Committee urged that students be given not only competence in one field of knowledge but access to related fields and a general appreciation of the art of learning. The Committee urged that students be helped to acquire interests outside their special subjects (para. 74). Again, in their next quinquennial statement (U.G.C. 1964, p. 105), the Committee declared that 'on the academic side, we declare our main interest to be in the general broadening of the undergraduate curriculum, in the breaking down of the rigidities of departmental organization, and in the strengthening of the relationship between teacher and taught'.

The Robbins Committee on Higher Education Report (Committee on Higher Education 1963), expressed concern about the excessive narrowing of students' areas of study. Noting that 40 per cent of those reading arts subjects at university took no science subjects (as distinct from mathematics) at G.C.E. ordinary level, and over one-third of those reading science took neither history nor geography at ordinary level, the Committee expressed their concern (p. 77):

We recognise that a combination of arts and science subjects for the Advanced level examination may provide a less coherent course than a combination of subjects within the science or within the arts fields. But there is no doubt that many boys and girls—particularly girls—would prefer broader courses in the sixth form and that this preference would be strengthened if, as we recommend later, there were a widespread development of broader courses at university level also. We are sure that many of those who go on to higher education would do better, both at school and later, if they had a less specialised education than the schools now feel obliged to give them. We do not believe, for example, that it is in the public interest that a student of natural science or technology is frequently not competent in even one foreign language, a student of economics is often without the desirable complement of mathematics and a student of history or literature may be unaware of the significance of science and the scientific method.

The Robbins Committee noted (p. 91) that although some students were very much at home in the single, specialized honours course, many young people would prefer broader studies provided that such courses carried no stigma of inferior status. They recognized that many students would like to enlarge their knowledge of a number of subjects and would feel constricted by the horizons of courses specializing in depth. In particular, the Committee discussed the needs of prospective teachers. A relatively high proportion of those graduating in the humanities enter the teaching profession, and the Committee noted that, with the prevailing shortage of mathematics teachers in particular, there is a good case for students who intend to go into teaching having available a wider course of study than is traditionally provided.

The *Enquiry into the flow of candidates in science and technology into higher education* of the Dainton Committee (Council for Scientific Policy 1968) expressed a similar concern, though for different reasons. Among the recommendations of the Dainton Committee were the following: that there should be a broad span of studies in the sixth forms of schools, and that irreversible decisions for or against science, engineering, or technology should be made as late as possible (para. 174); that normally, all pupils should study mathematics until they leave school (para. 179); that universities should reconsider their entry requirements with a view to encouraging a broad span of studies in the sixth form and to increasing the flow of candidates in science, engineering, and technology (para. 190); and that universities should consider further a range of courses designed to attract into science, engineering, and technology able students who are not already committed to these fields of study, but who are otherwise qualified to benefit from *ab initio* courses in these subjects at university level (para. 193). It is significant that the Dainton Committee recorded (para. 8), that although their enquiry began with the desire to correct the swing away from science in schools, this aim came to be seen as subsumed within the wider objective of meeting the needs of the individual pupil for a rounded education.

It might seem that the obvious way of achieving such a rounded education is to provide a general degree. However, it has long been recognized that the general degree suffers from a lack of prestige. The situation was well described by a speaker at the Home Universities Conference 1960 (Association of Universities of the British Commonwealth 1960, p. 31):

We find that the stamp of inferiority is definitely there in our general degree, and consequently this stamp of inferiority is cast over the whole idea of wider non-specialised study in the university. This might be all right if we found there was a strong demand for a sort of low grade degree, but we do not. The number applying for general is steadily dropping; we keep it alive at the moment only by a quota system . . .

Not only does the stigma of inferiority attach itself to general degrees which cover a mixture of arts and science subjects, but it also attaches to generalist degrees within one field or other. In their report on *The flow into employment of scientists, engineers and technologists* the Committee on Manpower Resources for Science and Technology (1968, pp. 77–8), discussed the problems raised by proposed reform of the first-degree course. The Committee noted that specialist undergraduate courses have acquired status and prestige throughout the whole educational system, whereas generalist courses are usually regarded as soft options, or as offering a lesser prize for those who fall behind in the specialist race. The Committee comment that the identification of subject specialization with academic distinction is not only inconsistent with breadth of learning and achievement found among those most eminent in their fields but that it may work against the best interests of the individual student.

It is in fact the social phenomena associated with the single-subject specialism that provide the principal constraints on any curricula reform in universities designed to provide for the science education of non-specialists.

6.1. The prestige problem

The Robbins Report gave formal recognition to a fact which is obvious to anyone in further education: namely, that in the minds of both students and teachers academic institutions are ranked with reference to each other in a very finely-graded prestige scale (Committee on Higher Education 1963, p. 9).

. . . it is inevitable that some institutions will be more eminent than others. It is in the nature of things that talent should attract talent and that where famous intellectual exploits take place, there should develop some concentration of staff and students especially interested in the subjects concerned. Moreover, such concentrations are not only probable but also desirable. A mutual stimulation of speculation and of scholarly standards is a precondition of much that is most valuable in higher education. It is therefore unavoidable that in this respect there should be some differences in achievement and reputation as between institutions. It is also unavoidable that because of the varying expense of different kinds of education and research different institutions should receive different subventions. What is important is that what differences there are should rest clearly on differences of function on the one hand, and on acknowledged excellence and the discharge of functions on the other. There should be no freezing of institutions into established hierarchies; on the contrary there should be recognition and encouragement of excellence wherever it exists and wherever it appears.'

It is paradoxical that the Robbins Committee applaud in this paragraph the very social phenomenon which most hinders the development of inter-disciplinary studies.

In their highly perceptive study Caplow and McGee (1958) show how high-prestige institutions seek to maintain their prestige. Staff are hired on an estimate of how much *research* they are likely to do; when their tenure is decided, direct utility to the university hardly enters as a factor in a decision to employ them and the measurement of their worth is haunted by quite another factor, their usefulness in *future staff procurement* (p. 92). The prestige of a department within a university is recognized by the contribution of its members to the furtherance of knowledge in the discipline which the department represents. The effect of this, as Caplow and McGee point out (p. 71), is that a scholar's orientation to his institution is apt to disorient him to his discipline and to affect his professional prestige unfavourably. Conversely, an orientation to his discipline will disorient him to his institution, which he will regard as a temporary shelter where he can pursue his career as a member of the discipline. There is therefore a choice between serving the institution by which a university teacher is employed (by teaching its students) and serving the discipline by publishing research. This conflict of roles sets up a situation of strain in which university teachers are paid to do one job—teach undergraduates—whereas the worth of their services to their institution is evaluated on the basis of how well they do in another job—publishing in their discipline. The career of a university teacher, unlike that of a schoolteacher, depends not so much on his teaching as on his research and so far efforts like that of the Prices and Incomes Board to redress this situation have been unsuccessful.

But, it might be argued, the British university system of the 1970s is not at all like the American one of the late 1950s. In their book *The British academics* (1971), Halsey and Trow have specifically contrasted the American and British situations (pp. 199–200):

> In particular energetic and competitive research activity may be relatively subordinate to those norms of academic life which place heavy emphasis on teaching and devotion to students—activities which do not necessarily enhance professional reputations.

Halsey and Trow later (p. 348) note that very few British academics, whatever their major subject or research interest, felt under 'a lot' of pressure to do more research than they wanted to. They comment that by and large the British university system seems able to accommodate teachers as well as researchers without placing much pressure on them to change their direction of interest. But when they discuss *promotion* Halsey and Trow find (p. 349) that emphasis on publication is felt to influence career opportunities: 'Disregarding subject, 32 per cent of our total sample "agree strongly" that promotion is "too dependent" on publication; and 76 per cent agree strongly or with reservations.' There are, of course, differences between what Halsey and Trow call 'teachers' and 'researchers'. Medicine apart, over 90 per cent of those who regarded their teaching duties as primary felt that publication weighed too heavily in promotion, as compared with between two-third and two-fifths of those who were primarily research-oriented.

Tenure of position is awarded earlier in British universities than in American ones. The salary structure is also 'homogenized' between institutions in the British system. These two facts probably account for the less feverish atmosphere in British universities, and the consequent possibility that some faculty members will devote themselves primarily to teaching. But there can be no doubt that 'disciplinary' prestige and the possibility of moving up the prestige pecking-order of institutions, largely depends not on a man's teaching ability but on his research 'productivity'.

For the university teacher, then, prestige and promotion are to be found principally through the mainstream activities of his department or sub-department. The pressures are, of course, strongest on the most junior members of staff, who normally serve a period of 'probation' of up to three years before being given positions of tenure. Junior university teachers, fresh from postgraduate work, are the most likely to be research-oriented. Not only have they recently acquired the taste for work at the limits of knowledge in their subject but they also need to demonstrate their research capability by publication—'publish or perish'. Having achieved tenure, they are highly likely to have adopted the ethos of the department or sub-department in which their research is carried out. This tendency is perhaps most strongly felt in science departments, where collaborative research often involving expensive apparatus is more common than in the humanities. An order of priorities rapidly becomes established: publication of research papers to further one's discipline (and at the same time one's own career opportunities); supervision of postgraduate students engaged in research similar to one's own—so that one may enlarge by personal contact one's knowledge of the frontiers of a subject; teaching of undergraduates in one's own discipline—preferably final-year honours students who may be expected to get first-class honours degrees and in turn become post-graduate students in one's sub-department; teaching of 'general studies' to undergraduates in other disciplines. Caplow and McGee (1958, p. 155) have enunciated a principle of the conservation of status. Gains of status, they maintain, are usually, but not always, sought by the incumbents of organizational positions; losses of status are always resisted. Caplow and McGee explore in great detail the effects on academic institutions of this principle, but for present purposes the effect on the willingness of science staff to teach non-specialists at university level is the most important one. This effect is almost entirely negative.

What is perhaps remarkable is not the *absence* of educational experiment but its very existence. The social forces favouring specialist study in the universities, and all the concomitant effects upon the school curriculum, are overwhelming. However, it is possible, as Bernstein (1971) has shown, to see what sort of professional ethic produces non-specialist courses. Bernstein starts from the premiss that how a society selects, classifies, distributes, transmits, and evaluates the educational knowledge it considers to be public, reflects both the distribution of power and the principles of social control. Bernstein distinguishes between two broad types of curriculum. He describes as a *collection* curriculum one in which the contents of the subjects studied are clearly bounded and insulated from each other; in contrast, an *integrated* curriculum is one in which previously insulated subjects or courses have been subordinated to some relational idea which blurs the boundaries between subjects. This description might be applied to the so-called 'integrated day' of the infant school in which pupils are encouraged to exercise systematic curiosity without much heed being taken of particular 'subject' labels. Bernstein shows how in the English version of education based upon the collection code, subject loyalty is systematically developed in pupils. Mixed categories such as biophysicists or psycho-linguists, are allowed to develop only after long socialization into a subject loyalty. In order for someone to change his identity, a previous one has to be weakened and a new one created. Bernstein notes that if a student in England has a first degree in psychology and wishes to read for a higher degree in sociology, either he is not permitted to make the switch or he is expected to take a number of papers at first-degree level in sociology. Bernstein argues that a sense of the sacred, the 'otherness' of educational knowledge arises not so much out of an ethic of knowledge for its own sake as from the process of socialization into subject loyalty. He maintains that any collection code involves a hierarchy of knowledge so that the ultimate mystery of a subject is revealed very late in the educational life of the individual—that is his potential for creating new realities. The ultimate mystery of a subject is shown to be not order but incoherence.

With integrated codes, the disturbance in the classification of educational knowledge leads to a corresponding disturbance of the existing specific educational identities of those brought up in subject loyalties and their associated concepts of property in knowledge. An attempt to subordinate subject content to some idea which reduces the isolation of topics involves, therefore, a challenge to social organization in the educational institution. Any move from a collection code to an integrated code is likely to bring a disturbance in structure and distribution of power, property relationships, and educational identities.

Bernstein argues that pedagogy in integrated codes is likely to emphasize *ways of knowing* rather than states of knowledge. For a curriculum of the integrated code type to succeed, Bernstein suggests that certain conditions need to be fulfilled. For example, there needs to be consensus about the integrating idea. Again, the nature of the link between the integrating idea and the knowledge must be spelled out. Working out the linkage is likely to produce its own form of socialization, and may depend upon a high degree of ideological agreement among those involved in the process.

Although Bernstein puts his ideas forward only tentatively, they provide an admirable explanation of the vigorous curriculum innovation in the new universities and former colleges of advanced technology in England particularly when these institutions were either small, or new, or both. Trow (1965), for example, reviewing *The idea of a new university* (Daiches 1964) expressed pleasure and surprise at the Sussex experiment. He suggested (p. 167) that Sussex may be swimming against the current in Britain: which he argues is for 'the mass processing of students, the triumph of the single-subject department and more highly organised post-graduate training'. Be that as it may, the vigour of curriculum experimentation in the new universities has included substantial experimentation in nonspecialist studies. Campbell (1964) has described in great detail the extent of this. What is of immediate interest in this book is the type of experiment carried out in science education for nonspecialists.

At the time of writing, some of the most interesting curriculum experiments in the science education of non-specialists at university level is being carried out by the Open University and by polytechnics offering courses for the approval of the Council for National Academic Awards. However, this chapter will be concerned with science for non-specialists in courses at universities.

6.2. Joint honours courses

Joint honours courses have a disinguished history in British universities; course like P.P.E. and 'Greats' are well-established in Oxford and courses in other universities are also becoming quite venerable. An idea of the staggering range and multiplicity of joint honours courses can be gained from perusal of the *Compendium of university entrance requirements* published by the Committee of Vice-Chancellors and Principals of the Universities of the United Kingdom (Association of Commonwealth Universities, annually since 1963). Most joint honours degrees combine subjects which are closely related, such as mathematics and physics, or English and history. Usually, students undertaking combined degrees which combine arts and science need science A-levels, and have to follow the same lectures as students majoring in the science. There are indeed some interesting combinations; music and physics at Glasgow, economics and engineering at Warwick and several other universities, philosophy or history of science and chemistry at Leeds, and so on. However, few universities drop the requirement of a science A-level for students undertaking such courses.

With the increasing tendency of sixth-formers to take a mix of G.C.E. A-levels including at least one subject in science, it is likely that these joint honours degrees will have a continuing market. However, joint honours degrees are not without hazard. Jevons (1969a, p. 157) has noted that it is all too easy for a university to set up a joint honours school merely by putting together halves of two existing honours schools. The danger of overloading becomes even greater than that in single-subject honours courses. Jevons comments that in general, but with some exceptions, joint honours courses are at once taxing and unattractive.

According to a correspondent in one university which offers a combined studies degree, cross-fertilization of disciplines and the adoption of a synthetic approach are not institutionalized in any formal sense and arise from the student's own approach to his fields of study; they should, it is thought, be evident in his outlook and completion of his combined studies degree course. At this university, there is no specific linking of the courses making up the combined studies degree and there is no pressure from the arts faculty for science grounding for students wishing to take science. The effective result is that very few students combine science with arts.

In another university, according to a correspondent, 'emphasis is placed especially on the ability of the student to integrate and compare the individual subjects ... an attempt is made to bring the various disciplines into a relationship'. But the 'attempt' was left to the students, and the effort at this particular university to provide a combined honours degree failed because most departments seemed either unable, or unwilling, to interrelate their disciplines with those of other departments.

When departments offering the joint honours degree remain behind their castle walls and the integrating effort is left to the students, the result can be not only an overload of work but intellectual incoherence or conflict. In the words of one graduate from a combined honours degree in mathematics and philosophy, 'It gave us intellectual schizophrenia. Each (subject) has its own methodology. The staff weren't interested in resolving the conflicts: we'd spend the morning in the philosophy seminar discussing how sets don't exist. Then we'd spend all afternoon *doing* them in maths.'

Perhaps the joint honours courses most likely to succeed are those which have some organizing principle. The honours course in 'human sciences' at Oxford University has such an organizing principle. The proponents of this course have argued (*Oxford University Gazette*, 7 August 1969) that

> The boundaries between many branches of biology, psychology, and the social sciences are becoming extremely tenuous, but development in these inter-disciplinary fields and a wider understanding of their importance is severely handicapped by the traditional definition of subject areas in university curricula and, particularly, by the continuing educational separation of the natural and social sciences.

The proponents of the course go on to explain that the subject of the Honours School of Human Sciences will be the biological and social aspects of the study of man. To this end, the relevant elements of genetics, ethology, ecology, psychology, geography, sociology, and anthropology are brought together in logical order. If the instigators of this integrated course can generate, sustain, and transmit the ideological agreement which Bernstein suggests is a prerequisite for such an activity, it would seem likely that it will succeed.

However, it remain true that joint honours courses at present do most for the science A-level student who wants to broaden his education, rather than for the arts A-level student who wants to broaden into science.

6.3. A special science and society course

Round every Senate table sit men for whom the word university stands for something unique and precious in European society: a leisurely and urbane attitude to scholarship, exemption from the obligation to use knowledge for practical ends, a sense of perspective which accompanies the broad horizon and the distant view, an opportunity to give undivided loyalty to the kingdom of the mind. At the same Senate table sit men for whom the university is an institution with urgent and essential obligations to modern society; a place to which society entrusts its most intelligent young people and from which it expects to receive its most highly trained citizens; a place which society regards as the pace-maker for scientific research and technological progress. And so universities find themselves searching for a compromise. (Eric Ashby, *Technology and the academics*, 1966, pp. 69–70)

Perhaps it would be unfair to call the honours degree in liberal studies in science of Manchester University a compromise in Sir Eric Ashby's sense of the word. It is, however, a new type of science degree which is not at present a course for the non-specialist but may eventually be thrown open to arts-stream applicants. Professor F. R. Jevons, the founder of the course, has written (1969*b*, p. 402): 'There can be no doubt that there exists a large all-rounder group of young people who are not incapable of science and technology but who are not prepared to devote themselves to that type of study with the degree of exclusiveness that most of the best education in this country at present demands.' To catch the so-called 'floating voters' Jevons suggests the possibility of a shift in emphasis in sixth-form and undergraduate courses towards cultivating the image of the scientist as the well-read scholar rather than the chap who gets himself dirty in the laboratory. Jevons attributes one of the attractions of arts courses to their style of teaching rather than their content. This style is reading-based, and by virtue of that, cultivates a critical attitude to printed matter.

Jevons questions what he calls the folklore tradition that arts graduates are more flexible and are better able to 'tackle anything' than science graduates because the numeracy barrier is a bigger limitation for arts graduates than anything that faces science graduates. Scientific training should, he argues, give more versatility but only if it provides comparable incentive and opportunity for the student to find out for himself about things by reading them up.

The model product of the liberal studies in science course which Jevons has started is what Bagrit (1965) called the science-oriented humanist. The course is designed for those who will interpret science to laymen.

Our graduates should be particularly qualified for a variety of key roles in the science-permeated society of the future—as teachers and journalists interpreting science to the public; as government or industrial administrators in areas with scientific content; and eventually as decision-makers who can assess not only the implications of policy for science but also those of science for the whole spectrum of public policies.

The course combines straightforward studies in physical science with studies of technology in the economic development of Britain since 1700, origins of modern science, social consequences of technology, case-histories of technological projects, science technology and politics, and scientists and society. At present, the entry requirements for the course include mathematics and physics at G.C.E.

I

A-level, though applicants with only one of these can be considered. If the course as at present constructed is successful in its objectives, it is likely to produce effective agents for the dissemination of science culture. If, as originally proposed, it eventually makes provision for those with arts A-levels it will provide an important university programme for the man who wishes to study some science without becoming a professional scientist or technologist.

Having considered joint honours courses and the liberal studies in science course, it is now time to turn to courses specially devised for students majoring in arts subjects.

6.4. Minority time studies

The courses described in this section of the chapter are ones specially designed to be taken by arts specialists in minority time. Such courses have been given at various universities under different titles such as distributed electives, distant minors, inter-faculty studies, etc. It is characteristic of this type of academic provision that it varies widely from year to year; therefore, the outline given in this chapter is not intended to be definitive but attempts merely to indicate the sort of thing that has been attempted.

The University of Lancaster, for example, provided for a breadth requirement for all its students. Arts students were able to take courses from the following list: principles of chemistry; outline of mathematical ideas; biology of man; principles of physics; techniques of operational research; sociology of religion; financial control; introductory analysis. A detailed account of one of these courses has been given by J. Heywood and H. Montagu-Pollock in an unpublished study: 'The teaching of the principles of physics to arts students: an experiment in curriculum development'. At the time described in this study, 1965-9, the breadth course contributed one-ninth of the student's maximum part II examination (or honours) mark. The principles of physics course was designed, in the authors' words, 'for the person who still has the 10-year-old's curiosity about the nature of the universe; who has views on whether Government officials, editors, or business executives need some knowledge of scientific ideas; or who considers that science could be as much part of our culture, as, say, the fine arts, but who is interested in principles rather than in detailed knowledge of a wide field'. The course consisted of lectures and practical work in physics and cosmology and had as its objectives: to illustrate the structure of thought and methods of inquiry of physics; to give students an insight into physics to such a point that they could increase their understanding unaided, when circumstances required it; to give students the opportunity for study in depth, and through changes in content and teaching method to increase their interest and maintain motivation; to enable students to compare the structure of thought and methods of inquiry in physics with those of their own subjects; and to show how the principles of physics were related to the problems of life.

At the University of Birmingham, every student has to include (usually in his first year) a term of lectures and seminars of inter-faculty studies. Seminar groups consist of approximately 10–16 students, each group meeting under the leadership of a member of staff. Seminar leaders are recruited from all the teaching staff, who receive invitations to take part in sections touching their own field, but may lead seminars in any section which appeals to them. Seminar groups are made up from the list of student choices and effort is made to include as wide a cross-section of faculties and departments as possible in each group. Students are required to write essays following attendance at inter-faculty studies courses, and the mark given to a student's essay (and an assessment of his performance in seminars) is entered on his record card. The weight given to this varies from department to department.

The aim of the inter-faculty studies is to contribute to a student's interest in matters of wide general importance which may lie outside the ordinary scope of his specialist work, and also to help him to fit his specialist work into its wider context in the larger pattern of science and learning. The courses are designed to encourage the student to read as widely as possible in a discriminating way. The inter-faculty studies course is divided into separate sections each with a different subject and generally consisting of nine weekly lectures and seminars for each section, each lasting one hour. In 1971, for example, the sections offered were as follows: The university and the community; the Soviet Union; what constitutes a city?; aspects of contemporary English drama; science and religion; arts and religion in ancient society; medicine and society; human origins; the computer; new developments in the arts. Students are given a free choice of these sections, with the proviso that a student is advised not to select a section whose subject approximates closely to the subject covered in his normal registered course. In practice, about one-third of the arts students take science courses; and two-thirds of the science and engineering students take arts courses. In the science and religion course, for example, 30 per cent of the participants were from combined studies or arts faculties; in the course on human origins, just over 21 per cent of the participants were from combined studies and arts courses; and in the course on the computer, only 15 per cent of students were from combined studies and arts faculties. It is therefore possible for an arts student effectively to avoid taking any serious science. Indeed, the choice of essay questions makes it possible for an arts student to deal with the sort of topic which might occur quite readily in his own discipline. For example, among the 1970–1 essay choices for the human origins course, was the following question: 'Man's emergence and his early societies'. Again, the course on the computer had the following essay options: 'The computer data-bank, a threat to personal liberty?' 'Discuss the likely impact of computers on society during the next ten years.'

Interestingly, inter-faculty studies have been the subject of extensive debate among staff and students at Birmingham University, culminating in a symposium on broader education on 5 November 1969 to discuss how the broader education component of the course might be improved. In January 1968, the Guild of Students Broader Education Committee issued a report commenting on inter-faculty studies in which they had several reservations about the effectiveness of the inter-faculty studies course as described above. First, the students emphasized that inter-faculty studies occupied only one term out of nine; even if the course succeeded in whetting a student's appetite for further study of the subject, he generally had no time to follow it up. The Guild felt it important that students should be able to follow up the course in their second and third years if they wanted to without detriment to their main courses. Secondly, the Students' Committee felt that inter-faculty studies had little prestige among students because they were a casualty of the intensive examinations system. With the heavy emphasis placed upon examinations, students were naturally hostile to any course that seemed to count little if anything towards their degree, despite the fact that inter-faculty essays were supposed to be taken into consideration. Thirdly, the students felt it to be the utmost importance that inter-faculty studies should give students ample opportunity to discuss subjects freely in seminars.

The students appreciated the difficulties that would be involved if their proposals were to be acted upon, particularly in administration and the pressures on staff (members of staff taking inter-faculty courses do so in their spare time). Fourthly, the extension of the inter-faculty studies course would also place a heavier burden on students, which in many cases could not be reconciled with existing courses. The students felt strongly that in such cases inter-faculty studies should not necessarily take second place. Summing up their views, the Students' Committee expressed serious concern that the University did not appear to be giving sufficient priority to consideration of the problems of broader education generally. They felt that there was a danger that the very existence of inter-faculty studies could divert attention from the more important aspects of broader education, relating to the nature of teaching, the examinations system, curricula, and university structure. The students felt that unless the Broader Education Committee was seen to be making a serious attempt to find a solution to the problems they had outlined, they would be in favour of the total abolition of inter-faculty studies on the grounds that their beneficial effects were insufficient to outweigh the fact that they enabled many departments to forgo their responsibility to ensure that their own courses provided for a reasonably broad education.

In similar vein, a staff *ad hoc* group for university reform produced a booklet *No easy answers; An analysis of the purposes of a university and imperatives of reform* (undated—?1969). This committee suggested that common first-year studies should provide the basis for 'inter-disciplinariness' in subsequent years. Issues raised in the first year would be followed through in their more particular applications to the student's chosen subjects or to his ultimate career. The Committee was convinced of the need for this continued pursuit of real scholarship by four main considerations (p. 25):

(i) New, more fruitful approaches often grow in the interstices of old 'disciplines'; (ii) many disciplines, in teaching and research, patently require elements of others to flourish and develop; (iii) existing provision for interdisciplinary studies (e.g., combined honours) are often unsatisfactory because they are artificial injections into a structure of autonomy which is perpetuated by departmental and faculty boundaries. The present course called 'inter-faculty studies' is inevitably little more than a palliative; (iv) real scholarship is vital to all our futures. Unless we can integrate the special, partial visions which existing disciplines represent, we will continue to live in a 'run-away world', victims of our own ingenuity. We refer in particular to the pathological divorce between the study of nature (natural science) and man's power over it (technology) on the one hand, and that of social relations (arts, social science and law) on the other. The resulting fragmentation of knowledge corres ponds to a practical failure to control the human environment.

The *ad hoc* committee commented that the fundamental difficulty was the absence of any real will among academics to learn about each other's work and the absence of an educational philosophy that makes this a meaningful pursuit. 'We may be sure that the links exist if only we search for them.'

This difficulty, as has been suggested above, is a feature not only of internal academic organization but also of the social features of the organization of knowledge. It is a reasonably safe generalization to say that behind any effective programme of inter-faculty studies such as those at Lancaster and at Birmingham stands a dynamic personality or group of personalities committed to the integration of knowledge. The vigorous debate at Birmingham (which still continues) is merely an illustration of the inevitable ideological clash between those who seek what Bernstein would call an integrated code of education in an institution dedicated to collection codes. The most effective types of integration of science into the curricula of arts students has taken place in institutions which are organizationally geared to doing this.

6.5. Freshman 'core' courses

Another approach to the assumed illiteracy of scientists and the supposed innumeracy of arts students has been the provision of common 'core' courses for first-year students. The University of Stirling, for example, which has a widely developed scheme of major and minor studies, has also experimented with a course in 'approaches and methods' which all students took during their first two semesters of their first year. According to the prospectus (1969–70, p. 17),

After a short initial period of instruction on information retrieval and the use of the library, the first semester of the course deals in general with the nature of language and its various uses. It introduces the basic ideas of logical appraisal and emphasises the application of logic as an analytical tool for clarifying both technical and ordinary language. It deals with imperfections in the use of language, with style and with communications media. The second semester covers the use of numbers, with an introduction to the computer, social arithmetic, problem analysis; uncertainty and games theory; scientific method, discovery and invention.

The thoroughness with which this course was conceived is evidenced by the production by the university of a special text *Words and numbers: A students' guide to intellectual methods* (ed. F. R. Bradbury 1969). Unfortunately, the course had to be abandoned owing to various institutional pressures, including the reluctance of some staff to conduct tutorials outside their areas of expertise.

At least one other course of similar design and intention folded up after two years at another new university. The story was communicated by one of its administrators.

This course was tried but discontinued. In the first year, lectures were given by practitioners of the various disciplines about the nature of their subject and seminars were held on the lectures directed by members of staff drawn from all subjects. Many students resented having to talk about things they thought they had managed to avoid for ever after 'O' levels. Seminars were not always very professionally conducted. Lectures on the whole were good; but became increasingly less well attended.

In the second year we tried something more like the Birmingham system of allowing students, after a series of introductory lectures, to opt for seminars in some special field. I think this was rather more successful. But, as our student numbers increased and staff time became more and more pre-empted by specialised work, staff became more and more reluctant to offer special courses, which would always be an additional, unpaid chore. We decided (the Committee dealing with the Course) that either it must be properly financed or terminated. It was not possible to finance it, so it was terminated.

If I were to get involved in such a project again, I should insist on one of two alternatives:

If there were to be any compulsion on students to attend the course, either as a mandatory part of the curriculum or for examination, it would be essential to have staff with some special expertise in dealing with such a course (or some special experience, such as extra-mural) for whom work on the course was a recognised part of their university duties. The course would then become demanding a portion of academic funds.

If the course were to be purely voluntary, I would take it out of the normal time-table period, and put things on at lunch-times ... or in the evenings. This again could not be done without a budget appropriation.

It is noteworthy that the most spectacular success in introducing science to non-specialists has taken place at the University of Keele, which is administratively prepared to cope with the task. Three factors seem crucial: first, that the university course for all students at present lasts for four years; secondly, that all students in the university are on combined courses of one sort or another; thirdly, that staff are recruited who are already committed to the idea of general education and whose contribution in this field is recognized and rewarded.

In brief, there are at Keele four ways in which non-scientists can do some science: first, through the foundation year in which all students attend a large programme of lectures covering many fields of human knowledge; secondly, through sessional courses (occupying the whole of the academic year) in which, for example, a student who has not passed in a natural science subject at G.C.E. Advanced level must take a course lasting the whole academic year from one of the natural sciences; thirdly, through subsidiary courses in subjects outside a student's main discipline which he takes in the years following the foundation year; and fourthly, through special encouragement to students taking the foundation year who wish to transfer from an arts background into a science major.

All students do the foundation year, which aims to introduce the student to the broad content of human knowledge and introduce him to the scope, methods, and inter-connections of many of the main branches of university study. About one-third of the course is scientific, the lectures being skilfully mixed with those in the arts and social sciences. At first sight, it might seem that the delivery of lectures in this kind of course would raise particular difficulties for science lecturers, since the audience of several hundred students contains some who may have taken physics and chemistry or mathematics at G.C.E. A-level, as well as those who have not even studied them to O-level. It is therefore a challenge to produce lectures which are both intelligible to the arts student and still interesting to the scientist. As one of the physics professors has written (Ingram 1966, pp. 255–6), 'Astronomy is particularly fortunate in this respect, since a great part of it can be presented in a qualitative fashion, which can be followed fairly readily by any intelligent arts student and, since it is not studied as such as a subject at school, the material can be sufficiently new to hold the attention of the scientists for most of the time.' Clearly this favourable phenomenon does not apply quite so clearly to other contributions that, say, physics makes in the foundation year course, but other ways are found of making the lectures intelligible on the one hand, and interesting on the other. In this respect, Ingram points out that stress is laid on the concepts behind scientific thinking and the implications and effects of scientific discoveries, since these are not points which are normally touched on in the traditional A-level syllabus, and they can be appreciated by both arts and science students alike.

The principal value of the foundation year is in giving an overview of human intellectual endeavour. It is in the sessional courses that deeper study can take place. In these sessional courses, arts students are introduced to practical scientific activity of the sort which Yudkin (1969) would recommend. By all accounts, this practical involvement with the concepts and activities of actual science is very stimulating. Iliffe (1968) has noted that no student whose previous education has concentrated heavily on arts subjects will become a scientist after twenty-five laboratory classes. What is accomplished in the sessional courses cannot be better conveyed than by an extract from a student's essay on the foundation-year course:

I feel that I have gained most this year from my sessional tutorials in physics—this was something completely new, and foreign to me; I have gained a gradual knowledge of the way in which scientists differ in their approach, the scope and methods of their work. It has also made me realise how unfounded was my former avoidance of mathematics and science, my feeling that arts and science require two different types of training, which could therefore not be compatible. These feelings have been replaced by a new enthusiasm for science in general and physics in particular; this in spite of the fact that I have gained little more than a glimmering of the basic laws of physics.

In addition to the sessional courses are the subsidiary courses through which all non-science students must qualify in science or mathematics as subsidiary studies in the first or second year after the foundation year, as well as in two subjects of their specialization and in another subsidiary subject which may be drawn from a subject closely related to their specialism. Once again, the involvement of students with practical scientific activity seems to be successful. Ingram has written revealingly of the reaction of students to taking subsidiary courses in physics (1966, pp. 258–9):

The reaction of the arts students to this subsidiary course (in physics) was one of my most interesting discoveries when first coming to Keele. I had imagined that they would be wanting and expecting rather vague and general lectures on such themes as 'The philosophy of physics' or 'The history of science' but these are not in fact the lectures which evoke much enthusiasm, mainly, one suspects, because they are so like the lectures that they already receive on the arts side. What was most impressive however, was to see the reaction of arts students when they were first introduced to practical experiments in the subsidiary laboratory. The real and genuine interest which they show on realising that here they can actually measure things for themselves and work out various properties from first principles is most encouraging and stimulating. There are, of course, the obvious traps and the difficulties in explaining to a large number of them why they cannot measure g to 5 significant figures by an experiment with a simple pendulum. But as soon as one sees the enthusiasm of an arts student for actually doing an experiment himself and getting a result from his own calculations, one knows that the otherwise insurmountable barrier between the arts and science outlooks is down, and some appreciation of the scientific method in action has come across in its most effective way. It is for this reason that all the science subsidiary courses for arts students lay particular stress on the need for practical work, since it is only by actually carrying out such experiments oneself that the full realisation of the methods and outlook of the scientist, and his need to appeal to observations as a final criteria, is thoroughly understood and appreciated.

One of the subsidiary advantages of the foundation year is that it gives students an opportunity, if they so wish, to change their subject of specialization when they become familiar with the aims, methods, and content of other disciplines. In fact, this facility results in a slight drift away from science in favour of, for example, social science subjects. Clearly, it is easier for a student to move this way than from a purely arts background into science, for the lack of science A-levels can be particularly inhibiting. However, it is probably one of the attractions of the foundation year course to members of specialist departments that through the foundation-year lectures they have the opportunity of attracting able students into their subjects. Indeed, the participation of subject specialists in the foundation year is a feature of the course which the University of Keele has maintained for reasons set out in Iliffe's report. The idea was discussed of having a special foundation-year staff group to build up a valuable body of experience in teaching and advising foundation-year students. Such staff could provide constant feedback for modifications in the foundation-year lecture course and could advise on examinations and other methods of assessment. Their experience might lead to changes to bring the sessional and term courses more in line with the overall aims of the foundation year. Every member of such a staff group would be able to attend *all* foundation-year lectures and could in time become conversant with all the recommended texts. It was argued that this might improve the guidance of discussion group work. Other members of the university staff would be relieved of some or all of their foundation-year teaching.

This last point, Iliffe argues, is probably the strongest consideration *against a* separate foundation-year staff group. The tendency of students to regard the foundation year as a curtain-raiser to their degree studies, rather than an integral part of them, would be increased by the separation of teachers into two corresponding categories. If tutors are prone to regard themselves primarily as departmental specialists and only incidentally involved in the foundation year, this attitude would equally be intensified. Again, recruiting staff to teach only first-year students might be difficult, and if it were not difficult, it would be dangerous, both to the individual tutor whose job would provide a challenge in teaching but little call for original scholarship, and to the university, with some 10 per cent of its staff in danger of academic immobility. So the balance of argument has been in favour of the contribution of all departments to the foundation year—a scheme which at present seems to be working remarkably well.

A further modification which has been suggested would be to divide the foundation-year intake into groups labelled arts and sciences and to teach them separately. The principal objection to this proposal is that to do this would reduce the basis on which students could discuss common problems, and would be likely to increase or at least maintain any prejudices of one group towards another brought with them from school. As it happens, the foundation year, taken jointly by students of all disciplines, seems to achieve the best features of the best school general studies, while at the same time avoiding the worst abuses of those studies.

The Keele programme, with its institutional acceptance, is an impressive model. However, since the Robbins Committee recommended that the duration of university courses should remain at three years, it is one which is not likely to be imitated in other universities. This is not to say that interdisciplinary activity cannot be practised; it is therefore appropriate to look at one more type of approach currently practised and to review possibilities for the future.

6.6. Interdisciplinary studies

Four techniques of injecting science into the university education of undergraduates have so far been reviewed. An important variant in method of approach is practised by some new universities, in particular the University of East Anglia and the University of Sussex. That is to have a scheme of Schools of Study which seek to subsume traditional departments in academic organization which recognizes interconnections and cross-fertilization between traditional disciplines. The scheme at the University of Sussex is, perhaps, a good case to examine because it has been widely publicized—for example by David Daiches (1963, 1964).

At the University of Sussex a student can study his major subject (economics, history, sociology, etc.) in the context of the work of a school in which he may share courses (called 'contextuals') with students taking other subjects as their main disciplines. For example, a student could major in economics in the School of Social Studies or in the School of European Studies. His major course of study would be the same in either case, but the contextual courses supporting it and forming a substantial part of his degree would be shared with students of other major disciplines studying in the same school. Although, by and large, the Schools of Studies are divided between the arts and social studies on the one hand and the sciences on the other, it is possible for students to take major parts of their degree courses in subjects which cross disciplinary boundaries. For example, engineers may study social psychology and economics, or geography may be studied as a major subject in the School of Biological Sciences. In addition to this system of overlapping schools, there is a programme known as the arts–science scheme which deliberately crosses the confines of an undergraduate's School studies. In it, arts undergraduates must take some account of the methods and results of the sciences, and science undergraduates consider the historical, social, or philosophical aspects of scientific work or make a study of a different topic in the humanities of their own choice. There is no doubt that students have thus been exposed to ideas and information which they might otherwise have been innocent of. Here, for example, are some titles of dissertations written under the arts–science scheme by students in the School of Educational Studies: 'Animal societies'; 'Chemical and biological warfare'; 'Evolution, genetics and aggression in Man'; Hormones and behaviour'; 'Genetics'; 'Alchemy—science, philosophy or religion?'; 'The hypothetico-deductive method of scientific enquiry'; 'The solar system: its nature and origins'; 'Personality, physique and ability in sport'; 'The techniques of art restoration'.

However, the arts–science scheme has been considerably modified since its inception. One can trace small, but crucial, modifications of the scheme in successive issues of the University's annual report. In 1962–3, for example, the report records that there was considerable discussion during the academic year on ways and means of introducing arts subjects into the science curriculum, and vice versa. More than half the members of the teaching faculty agreed to co-operate in the holding of joint arts–science seminars for all undergraduates; these seminars would constitute the second phase of the three-phase programme. The first phase would consist of a special series of lectures for both arts and science students on topics of common interest, to be delivered in the third term of the first year. The seminars would be held in the first term of the undergraduates' second year and would cover a wide range of subjects at various meeting-points of the arts and sciences. In the third phase, science students would be expected to produce dissertations on arts subjects of their own choice. The 1963–4 report recorded considerable progress in the implementation of the arts–science scheme. However, a modification is seen in the report for 1965–6: the programme of work pursued under the arts–science scheme continued this year to concern itself mainly with second-year undergraduates. The organization of the seminars in the autumn term recognized explicitly that students in science schools and arts schools might require different background discussion and topics. The seminars were therefore designed to start a trend towards covering mainly arts topics for the scientists and science topics for arts students. However, several seminars (some with an associated lecture course) were provided for mixed groups of arts and science students.

By the time of the report for 1966–7, the scheme had started to yield to disciplinary pressures. The report noted 'some evolution towards a new structure'. One such change (extended from the previous year) was the provision of an almost completely separate set of seminars for science students and for arts students: very few seminars consisted of a mixed group of arts and science students. Science students, in all schools except applied sciences, attended seminars in the autumn and spring terms covering a range of topics in arts and social studies. They continued their work by preparation of their dissertations; and as in previous years, they were allowed a free-ranging choice of dissertation topic. In order to take account of increased examination pressures throughout the second year, and also in clearer recognition of the nature and role of such a piece of work for the science student, the dissertation was reduced in length from 5000–10 000 words to 3000–5000 words. The report went on to say that arts and social studies students were offered a limited number of seminars by members of the science faculty. 'The continued absence of any form of degree-requirement for their arts–science work, and the lack of integration of such seminars with the student's other course work, meant that set seminars operated under some severe disadvantages.'

By 1967–8 the mixing of arts students and science students in joint seminars seems to have been abandoned. The report records as follows:

Undergraduates now fulfil the requirements of the Arts–Science programme in one of two ways depending on their degree. Some undergraduates pursue multi-disciplinary degree courses which basically involve considerable participation by both arts and social studies faculty members and science faculty members. Examples include undergraduates majoring in geography, psychology, philosophy and theory of science, etc. Such students are deemed to have fulfilled the requirements of the Arts–Science programme in the course of their ordinary degree work.

For all other undergraduates, a special arts–science programme continued to be provided.

Although the arts–science scheme remained a strong feature of the Sussex programme, other signs were apparent that parts of the programme were now becoming increasingly part of the property of the schools. For example, a letter about science for arts undergraduates addressed to students in the School of European Studies in May 1969 explained the University's policy that undergraduates in arts should learn something about the ideas and methods of science, as science undergraduates on their side learn something of the world of arts and social studies. It mentioned the University's compulsory arts–science programme and went on to say 'recently the whole programme has been overhauled, and the schools have taken charge of its content, structure and timing. From now on the arts undergraduate will be responsible to his school for his science course, as he is for his other courses.' For students in the School of European Studies who had not satisfied the University's requirement for science through their major studies, five special science courses had been worked out 'which would be taught in seminars by members of the science faculty in consultation with colleagues on the arts side. Each course may be regarded as a scientific extension of particular courses which you will already have done or will be doing later. The work done in these seminars, though not comparable to major or contextual papers, will be taken into account in your finals.' The courses are then listed as: (i) European cosmologies; (ii) The scientific revolution (Renaissance to eighteenth century); (iii) Modern science and the image of man, nineteenth–twentieth century; (iv) Science, technology and society in modern Europe; (v) The architecture of molecules.

Although it is dangerous, imprudent, and perhaps rude of the outsider to comment, it does seem that the pressures of the academic market-place are making themselves felt on the Sussex programme. Once again, Bernstein's analysis seems highly appropriate. An integrated programme, like the arts–science scheme, flourished splendidly in the early years of the university when the student population was relatively small, and the faculty were united by a common educational ideology. However, as the university grew in size, and the influence of the founding fathers became less pervasive, it is possible to detect the establishing of 'property rights' in the syllabus, and the withdrawing of academics into their schools. In other universities, Sussex is renowned for the heavy teaching demands made upon its staff, but this renown may be totally unjustified for the faculty of Sussex University are no less distinguished in what Caplow and McGee call research 'productivity' than members of other universities. It will be interesting to see if the educational–social structure of the university can maintain the interdisciplinary programme in the face of the 'publish or perish' pressures to which academic staff (particularly at junior level) are inevitably exposed.

6.7. Some other possibilities

From what has already been said, it should be clear that in universities which are not so heavily committed, in every way, as Keele is to broad education, minority options tend not to be taken seriously by staff or by students. The success of some existing schemes is largely due to the presence of enthusiasts, and one wonders what will happen when the enthusiasts leave. As the director of one highly successful scheme of interdisciplinary studies said in conversation: 'One's permanent nightmare is that the student will turn to you after a closely worked-out course and say "so what?" '

Basically, the pressures acting against science as a minority study in the university education of non-specialists are of two sorts: pressures on the student, and pressures on the faculty members. It is difficult to see how the pressures on the faculty members in a highly competitive career situation can readily be eased. However, various devices have been proposed which would ease the pressure on undergraduates by offering them the opportunity (with suitable reward) for extending their horizons. As it happens, the two types of pressure are interdependent, for whatever course is offered to the students, it must still be taught, and if teachers are more attracted to research and publication, no amount of administrative manipulation is going to change the basic situation. It is, none the less, worth examining two more possible ways of broadening the arts specialists' education into the realm of science.

The first possibility is to modify the entire structure of university degrees so that the first (bachelor's) degree would become a generalist degree and not a specialist one as at present. If the proportion of students taking a mix of G.C.E. Advanced levels continues to grow (see Council for Scientific Policy 1968, fig. 5, p. 13), there might be a considerable interest among students in a broad type of first degree spanning a range of subjects. Pippard has proposed a novel pattern of university education for the intending scientist or engineer (see Annex E of the Committee of Manpower Resources for Science and Technology Report (1968) and Pippard (1969)). The basic feature of Pippard's proposal is for a first (bachelor's) degree lasting only two years, after which some students would wish to leave the university, followed by a master's degree lasting for a further two years. In the master's degree, the student would undertake a very much more specialized course than at present, and this in turn should be followed by further study for those who intended to proceed to a Ph.D. Although the scheme is designed primarily for scientists and engineers, the model would be equally applicable to the university studies of arts specialists. Only a relatively small number of institutions would carry out the advanced teaching. This recognizes, and institutionalizes, the concept of centres of excellence, which whether academically desirable or not is a social fact. However, from the point of view of educating undergraduates, the scheme more or less suggests that general education, however desirable, is something to be 'had' and got out of the way as early as possible— rather like measles. The real problem is avoided, not solved. What is needed is some way of ensuring that arts specialists at university maintain contact with science culture throughout their lives, and are rewarded for doing so.

Another device would be to alter the methods by which students are assessed in order to recognize their participation in studies which were not within their academic major. Elton (1968) has described a scheme in which students obtain credits as well as marks for work undertaken in the degree. A credit rating is attached to a particular course in terms of the time involved in taking it and the difficulty of it. In the scheme which Elton (1968, pp. 295–6) describes, a student can obtain credits in two basic ways. The first is for courses that are not examined in the final examinations, such as general studies. Full credits are awarded if it is considered that a student has profited sufficiently from a course to enable him to tackle a continuation of this or a similar course in the next stage of his degree. Half credits are awarded for a performance that is somewhat below this standard. In the scheme, the full credit standard is no better than a marginal pass. Elton comments that this is as it should be, since credits are a measure of *course content* and not of a student's success. Credits can also be obtained for courses that are examined in a final examination: full credit is given for attendance at the examination. The credit rating of course depends on the difficulty and length of the course taken.

Elton emphasizes that the criteria for credits in no way depend upon the marks which the student accumulates through course-work and examinations. This feature, by which a student obtains full credits by simply showing that he has profited adequately from the course makes it essentially different from the American scheme and, Elton argues, avoids the feeling in the student that he has to stretch

K

himself to the fullest in whatever he does. In Elton's scheme, the more credits a student has amassed, the longer and harder his course has been, and the lower should his final percentage marks be for a given class of honours degree; at the same time, the course content must not drop too low for a given class of degree. Cut-offs can be fixed below which a student cannot obtain a given class however high his percentage mark.

In the experience of those who tried out the scheme of credits and marks at the University of Surrey, credits provided a satisfactory reward for students and an incentive to them. They also have the singular advantage that they can be awarded for work in subject areas which are regarded as valid in the education of the student but where the reliability of marking is low. Again, such a scheme could clearly be used to reward students for undertaking activities which might be outside what they regarded as their normal range of competence, but which the university deemed valuable for their education, in such a way that poor performance would not drastically lower their chances of achieving a high class of honours in the degree. In a way, the scheme is rather like that of offering trading stamps for produce bought. The analogy holds, because if there is no produce to be bought, trading stamps cannot be acquired.

7 *Science in Broadcasting*

ALTHOUGH education is the chief method by which cultural values are transmitted, there are obviously many others. The National Lending Library of Science and Technology takes over 36 000 separate periodicals and files away each year over 1 000 000 scientific papers. Specialist journals cater for every conceivable sector of the scientific fraternity, and several journals (for example, *New Scientist*) are directed at educated sectors of the general public. However, by far the biggest potential audience for science is found in broadcasting. More than 90 per cent of the British population have television sets in their homes; even more have access to radio. It is not unusual for a science programme on television to be seen by between five and six million people—more, in fact, than attend all the meetings of the British Association for the Advancement of Science in the course of an entire year. Even an intellectually demanding broadcast on Radio 3 will be heard by between 50 000 and 200 000 persons. This chapter will examine some of the objectives of science broadcasting, the techniques used in pursuing them, and the pressures on those whose job it is to broadcast science. Further Education broadcasts draw such small audiences that little is known about the public they attract; the Open University is directed to a specialized audience. Again, educational broadcasts directed at schools present a special case. This chapter is therefore concerned with science in general broadcasting. Television and radio have different potentialities and limitations, and will be dealt with separately.

It is difficult to disentangle the science in television from everything else that goes on there. What, for example, are the television space-spectaculars from the moon? They contain elements of pure

K2

journalism and show-business mingled with serious discussion of scientific phenomena and technological problems. They are partly news stories telling who did what, when, why, and where and partly live adventure stories focusing attention on the deeds of heroes. Any general appreciation of the activity of scientists and engineers and any understanding of general physical laws is probably incidental to the drama of these occasions. But are they, therefore, unsatisfactory science broadcasting?

Probably the richest ground in which seeds of curiosity can be sown is the broadcast which engages attention by several devices of television technique simultaneously. J. Scupham, sometime Controller of Educational Broadcasting in the BBC, has argued that there should be no sharp boundary between general interest programmes and programmes designed to open up new horizons: 'Science in the garden is still science' (Scupham 1967, p. 131). Again, Wedell (1968, pp. 165–6) has argued that categorization of programmes and audiences tend to destroy creativity in television. Considerable burdens of science fact may be borne by programmes of science fiction or dramatic series about doctors. But, clearly, if science, like art and music, is to be part of the general culture, it should not have to hitch-hike on news items about space stunts or headline-hitting river pollutions. How, then, does science occur in general broadcasting?

Aubrey Singer (1966, p. 15), former head of BBC Television Science and Features, has stated the aim of science broadcasting as 'to create a climate of critical opinion, in which the work of the scientist can be understood, encouraged, and criticized so that the body politic can intelligently share in and influence the course of science, directly through government, and indirectly by informed comment and discussion.' But a climate of opinion cannot be created against the wishes of those who are going to hold the opinion; the BBC must have the interests of its audience first in the order of priorities. National interest or the interest of particular sections of the scientific community are secondary. 'No matter how important, nationally or locally, a notion may be to any group that may be backing it, if it does not find favour with the audience in terms of broadcasting then it does a disservice both to the original idea and, even more important, to the audience itself (op. cit., p. 13). The BBC's charter proclaims the Corporation's duty to inform, entertain, and educate; few programmes which fail to entertain are likely to get very far with the audience. Recognition of this is not an article of policy, but deference to the facts of life. Lord Reith's dictum that 'few people know what they want and fewer still what they need' was not arrogant paternalism, but merely a statement of fact. Robert Silvey, former head of BBC Audience Research, has explained how the dice are loaded against any programme which stretches the mind or the imagination, which calls for thinking rather than feeling. Very few viewers really want to share in and influence the course of science; viewing, Silvey argues, is a form of play which takes place at home where people are relaxed. The average viewer is largely uncritical of what is on.

Because viewing is play, at home, and for nothing, one of the pleasures it offers is that of not having to make decisions. Hence some viewers will always, and most viewers will sometimes, not so much choose as drift, taking the line of least resistance. This may result in the set being 'left on' to whichever channel it happens to be tuned or to the effective abdication of the right to choose in favour of a set of invariable habits.

The frame of reference in which television viewing takes place for most people is not one of an earnest desire for self-betterment. 'If you are only out to enjoy yourself, why do it the hard way?' Programmes calling for mental effort, and particularly ones containing potentially disturbing new ideas, may threaten the viewers' assumptions. 'By contrast, programmes which make few demands upon viewers, and above all those which are built into a cosy framework of familiarity, minister positively to the needs for reassurance and emotional security which are in some sense universal' (Silvey 1962). It is, then, to a relaxed and relaxing audience that science programmes have to be directed.

Singer (1966, p. 14) has explained how science programmes are designed to be 'entertainingly informative at an intellectual level'. The need to be entertaining—to hold an audience large enough to support the broadcasters' morale—does not rule out seriousness. When scientists are asked to tell their story, an audience of equals in intelligence is assumed; an audience well disposed towards, but with no special knowledge of, the subject-matter. People may enjoy a programme without necessarily understanding it; they will be satisfied if they feel they have gained some insight into a subject, if their curiosity has been aroused, or if their confidence in an activity has been increased. But the need to be guided by the logic of the broadcast situation, rather than the inner logic of a science, has some important implications for the sort of science which can be made popular through television.

How does a particular programme get on to the air? The initiative comes from individual producers. In Independent Television programmes are set up by the programme-making companies under the general heading of documentaries, as news, or occasionally as special features. The BBC has a Science and Features Department which is specially concerned with science programmes. The BBC also has a Science Consultative Group which meets twice a year to proffer advice and suggestions. The group, which was formed following a recommendation of the Pilkington Committee, consists of distinguished scientists. One experienced broadcaster, Stuart Hood, has written that 'is is good for the souls of programme-makers to be exposed from time to time to advisory committees'. But he doubts whether many worth-while programme ideas ever originate from the deliberations of the committees (Hood 1967, p. 48). The individual members of the committees are, however, likely to be part of the huge informal network of contacts through whom the programme-makers keep in touch with what is going on in the frontier-outposts of science. Sherry poured into the right glass on the right day, a telephone call to get more information about an item in a specialist journal which has caught a producer's eye, hearing an exciting exposition of an abstruse idea at a scientific congress—these and many other movements of sensitive antennae result in programmes being generated. From the initiative of a producer or the head of the science unit, an idea for a programme will go to the programme controller for a particular television channel if the programme is competing for time with other possible programmes—for example, as a Tuesday documentary. Or, a producer will be asked to make a programme to fit into one of the regular television science and technology series, such as 'Horizon' or 'Tomorrow's World'.

It is then that all the pressures of the broadcast medium come to be felt at their strongest. George Gerbner (1969) has charted in some detail the range of these pressures among which may be noted: pressures from clients who supply funds; from supervisors of policy; from colleagues; from competitors; from auxiliaries who supply commodities or control distribution. These pressures are felt most strongly in commercial television where income depends upon the size of audience which can be attracted. Television is highly expensive: upward of £5000 an hour is the usual conservative estimate of the broadcasting authorities. If funds from advertisers cannot be attracted, commercial television cannot function. Programme controllers therefore have to weigh science programmes against others likely to hold the audience. Even the BBC, which is immune from these direct commercial anxieties, has pride in competing with the Independent Television Authority for the attention of viewers.

Then, the intangible pressures from colleagues make themselves felt. Producers are busy men with high standards of artistic self-discipline. There is a dangerous tendency to produce for one's colleagues in, say, the Television Centre, and to ignore audience research reports and to get out of touch with housewives in Huddersfield. Again, in vast organizations, there is a tendency to compete with one's colleagues for the honours of the air. As Mary Adams, former head of BBC Talks, has observed: 'Competition does not help a rational approach; producers, irrespective of their allegiances, fish in the same professional waters . . .' (Adams 1959).

Quite apart from these pressures, there are those of time. A producer of a 45-minute edition of 'Horizon' has only thirteen weeks from the start of the operation to the screening of the finished programme. Four or five weeks may have to be devoted to research on the subject, finding what ideas are important in the science and from these which ones are communicable by television; another week may be spent in choosing locations for filming, another week or more in filming. Editing is a time-consuming and demanding process and involves not only technical skill but infinite diplomacy in handling scientists who may feel that the omission of some slab of unviewable material completely undermines the authority of a viewpoint. In an article on 'Television producer and scientist' (1969, p. 457), Reid has noted that this sort of situation is regrettable but unavoidable:

The producer is doing what he is paid for: exercising his power of judgment. It is never possible to assess the success or otherwise of a recording until it is projected as a piece of film or edited in the context for which it was intended. Rejection is irritating not only for the participant, it is disagreeable for the producer; it reflects on his powers of judgment, and it is expensive.

In the same article (p. 458), Reid has described the process of editorial control of broadcast material, and has also argued that programme content must be the responsibility of broadcasters and not necessarily of the scientists who contribute :

> It must be emphasised that if, as a general principle, all those who take part in a programme were consulted in detail on how their contributions should be edited, there would be no end product. Television programmes, like plays, books, journalism, scientific research, paintings and literary criticism, cannot be produced by a concourse of opinion; time, economics, artistic and many other reasons totally exclude this. Concourses of opinion seldom exist (sometimes on matters as apparently incontrovertible as scientific fact); there comes a time when debate and adjustment must stop, and when the decision to publish—to transmit— must be taken.

Reid argues that if the scientist took over the responsibilities of the producer, he would effectively become 'the broadcaster'. If he is to carry out this new role adequately, he would have to acquire the professional skill and experience of a producer, and devote a producer's time and energy to the programme. In doing this, he would cease to be a scientist; he would, in effect, have become a producer.

Considering the difficulties faced by the producers and programmers it is a wonder that the messages of journalism and show-business do not swamp the science every time. In *Science and the public mind* Wilbur Schramm (1962) has shown how journalists tend to seek the personal or sensational in material. What he says of science writing is also true of television science :

> If you can put something in story form it will be read by more people. If you can make it apply to the reader, more will read it. If you can be concrete and specific, rather than abstract and general, more people will read it. If you can stress the sensational elements, it will be read by more people. If you can personalise it, it will be more widely read. This applies to both personalising the meaning of the story and personalising the author.

Schramm has noted how the mass media use journalistic techniques in reporting science and select material which can be so treated.

At worst, this journalistic approach can result in the twisting of the science, which is covered to fit some image of audience expectations in the mind of the broadcasters. Tannenbaum (1963) reports some interesting research carried out by Johnson (1961) in which it appeared that some American editors had an image of their audiences' expectations which corresponded very poorly indeed with the audiences' actual expectations. A selection of forty diversified specimens of science writing were judged by groups of scientists, science writers, newspaper editors, readers of science news, and people who did not normally read science news. The results of this exercise were very revealing. Four of the five groups made similar judgements as to the value of the pieces of writing which they read. The one group that deviated from the pattern and exhibited a unique factor was the group of editors. Where the scientist, science writer, or science reader considered a science news story valuable independently of whether he considered it exciting, the editor was more likely to value an item if it was considered exciting. It appeared that, for the group of editors, what was exciting was good—almost by definition.

One other finding of Johnson's study is worthy of note. He found that, contrary to the rather general assumption that readers are not necessarily interested in science *per se* but are interested only in results and applications, the study showed that stories which dealt mainly with pure research were valued more than those that dealt mainly with applications. This finding held true not only for the scientists in the sample but also for the readers and, to a lesser extent, those who were not traditionally readers of science news.

However, the tendency noted by Schramm of journalists to personalize news and show its application to the lives of the audience, has its positive side. A survey carried out by the Institute for Social Research at the University of Michigan on the public impact of science in the mass media (Davis 1958) demonstrated that public interest in science was directly related to the way in which it affected the individual. Similar conclusions may be drawn from the study *Science and the mass media* by Kriegbaum (1968). Medical topics, in particular, which of course directly affect the individual, seem to have a singular power of attraction. If one of the justifications for scientific activity is its value to the individual and to the community, the pressure which is experienced by broadcasters to demonstrate the relevance of science to the community may be a very valuable one.

What is less satisfactory is the journalistic pressure to emphasize the new and the show-business pressure to emphasize the spectacular or the journalistic *and* show-business pressure to stress issues involving human conflict. Nature programmes like 'Look' show that observation of the ordinary can make excellent television. Norman Swallow (1966, p. 26) has observed:

> Not only can audiences be 'trained' to enjoy serious programmes, but also a new generation is growing up which actively wants such programmes. Current affairs television, like so much else in the world of entertainment, has sometimes suffered from the impresario's tendency to underrate his audience, to play safe until the point where the public has not only caught up with him but is way ahead of him.

If this is true of current affairs, it is almost certainly true of science broadcasts. An audience of half a million viewers followed an austere and demanding series of talks by Professor Hermann Bondi on relativity. This is a pretty sizeable 'minority' by any standards, and, as Scupham has noted, at a cost per head of roughly one new penny per lecture, this series was hardly an extravagant use of television resources.

The BBC has tried some boldly imaginative experiments in science television. Programmes like the marathon $2\frac{1}{2}$-hour 'The violent universe' cannot be made every week (indeed, as Reid (1969) notes, it took 30 weeks of preparation), but a good precedent has been set by this large-scale programme on an intensely interesting and complicated subject. Perhaps only an organization as relatively flexible in its policies and as free from the financial need to gain big audiences as the BBC could have attempted such a programme. Indeed, it is difficult to see how such an expensive television project, taxing alike to producers and to viewers, could be attempted if earning quick money was the prime consideration. Williams (1968, p. 32) has deplored the '. . . dependency on advertising money, which leads to a policy of getting a large audience as quickly as possible to attract and hold advertisers. . . . All the basic purposes of communication—the sharing of human experience—can become subordinated to this drive to sell.' The plant which can produce such splendid fruit as 'The violent universe' is, indeed, a very tender one.

But however bold the broadcasters may be, there is one serious limitation in television: it is bad at presenting abstractions, simply because it is a visual medium. Hood has noted (1967, p. 132) that

> the success of programmes dealing with surgery—apart from their appeal to our basic hypochondria—is precisely that they demonstrate a kind of manual skill—the surgeon dilates the valves of the heart, a gall-stone springs out of a man's guts, a child is born. These are all practical

demonstrations as matter of fact, in their own way as plumbing or putting together an electrical circuit. General statements are more difficult to convey.

This is where radio comes into its own.

Apart from the fact that the temptation to fish for competitive audiences is absent, radio lends itself to treatment of a subject in greater depth. Much radio broadcasting has come to be regarded as 'musical wallpaper', background noise to accompany a range of other activities. Most Britons listen to the radio at some time during the day, but usually while they are doing things at home or riding in their cars. Nevertheless, serious science talks, often up to an hour or more in length, attract audiences comparable to those for serious music—in the range 50 000–200 000. As radio is only one-fifth to one-eighth as expensive as television, this is a perfectly acceptable figure.

As with television, so with sound radio: the aim of science broadcasting is to communicate not just information, but pleasure and entertainment as well. Dr. Archie Clow, formerly head of the BBC Radio Science Unit, has stated very clearly the criteria by which he would assess the suitability of a topic for broadcasting and the performance of a scientist as broadcaster (Clow 1956). There are four:

(a) The scientist must have something to say: this doesn't necessarily correlate with the desire to broadcast; (b) there must be a valid reason for letting the public know about the topic in which he is an expert ... ; (c) the scientist must be able to treat his topic in an imaginative way: he must not deliver research reports. The speaker must write to communicate, not just to publish, and must get away from the 19th century attitude: 'Here are my results, take them or leave them.' (d) He must be able to perform from the script. In the end a broadcast is an act; but showmanship must not override the requirement of scientific accuracy.

It is because broadcasting is an act that the policy—and of course the techniques—of science broadcasting must remain fairly and squarely with the broadcasters themselves. Even when the 'grand old men' of science are used as speakers in science broadcasts, tape-editing and stop-watches must play their part.

Scientists may bemoan the fact that the science unit of BBC radio is smaller than the religious broadcasting department. They may be horrified that in a sample week's television (cf. Williams

1968, p. 67) science fact programmes commanded 1 hour 10 minutes on BBC 1 compared with 14 hours of sport, 3 hours 40 minutes of crime and espionage, and 2 hours 25 minutes of Westerns. If scientists were more anxious to tell people what they are doing, no doubt more time could be found if the broadcasts seemed likely to be interesting. The Radio Science Unit receives very little unsolicited material, and the television programme-makers are always eager for ideas. What is perhaps most surprising in the whole field of science broadcasting is how little is actually known about what people want from science broadcasts.

The BBC Audience Research Department regularly samples audience reaction to programmes (see BBC 1970) but very few 'before-and-after' studies are carried out to measure the effectiveness of a broadcast in dispelling ignorance or arousing interest. By and large, the Audience Research Department does not have the authority—nor, more important, the funds and personnel—to carry out such studies. Again, producers rushing to meet deadlines have little time to devote to such matters. Occasionally a study will be carried out on a series of broadcasts. In *The impact of television*, Belson (1967, ch. 8) describes the impact of a series of broadcasts about mental health on the beliefs, knowledge, and attitudes of viewers. But nothing appears to have been done in Britain comparable to the Michigan survey, *The public impact of science in the mass media* (Davis 1958). There is a clear need either for a strengthening of the audience research services of the BBC or for some study carried out by an independent agency with co-operation from the BBC and the Independent Television Authority.

The chief characteristics of broadcasting are, perhaps, best summed up by Wright (1960, p. 606), who has defined mass communications as:

... directed towards relatively large and heterogeneous audiences that are anonymous to the communicator. Messages are transmitted publicly; are timed to reach most of the audience quickly, often simultaneously; and are usually meant to be transient rather than permanent records. Finally, the communicator tends to be, or operate within, a complex formal organisation that may involve great expense.

The two points which need most emphasis are the heterogeneity of the audience and the transience of the message.

Independent television depends on its advertisers; BBC television is paid for from the licence fees of *all* set owners, not just those interested in science. In both services, the programme-makers have to create a delicate balance between providing what they know the audience want or need and what they think the audience *ought* to want and need; between aiming to please all of the people all of the time (which might lead to mere pap) or most of the people some of the time. That so little is known about what audiences really want can only be deplored. The power of radio and television to excite interest and set people off on independent personal lines of inquiry is immense. Booksellers and librarians are aware of the sudden demand precipitated by the televising of, for example, a dramatization of part of a Victorian novel. Again, the institutional pressures upon broadcasters to emphasize the relevance of science to the individual and to the community (an influence stemming from broadcasting's origins in show-business and journalism) are a positive force in the absorption of science into general culture. Well-organized programmes of general education in science for highly articulate non-specialists, as described in Chapters 5 and 6, have their place; but the broadcasting of science programmes to a heterogeneous audience, consisting not only of university graduates but also of pupils who left secondary school after taking the Certificate of Secondary Education, presents a formidable and fascinating challenge.

It may be the transience of broadcasting that makes scientists reluctant to involve themselves in the time-consuming rough-and-tumble of programme-making. To give one's name to a constant or to a 'law', to achieve membership of the Royal Society, and to be recognized through one's specialism in an international community of scientists, may be more attractive than telling tax-payers what one is doing and why. Radio and television producers, the key men in the broadcasting process, depend upon the willingness of scientists to participate in programmes—indeed, to take initiative in pressing ideas upon them. At present, the popularizing of science is an activity of relatively low prestige. Perhaps the broadcasting authorities could take the initiative in arranging some TV series, comparable to the Reith Lectures on sound radio, to which high prestige would become attached.

Whenever the institutions of science in the United Kingdom have become remote from the interests of ordinary people, other institutions have arisen to take over the responsibility and prestige.

When the Royal Society, at the end of the eighteenth century, was becoming rather remote as a learned society, the Royal Institution was founded by Count Rumford. The Royal Institution has a distinguished history in meeting its founder's intentions in, for example, 'bringing forward into general use new inventions, and improvements, particularly such as relate to the management of heat and the saving of fuel and to various other mechanical contrivances, by which domestic comfort and economy can be promoted'. By 1831 it had become a meeting-place of the intelligentsia and has continued to this day to be one of the few places of high prestige where distinguished scientists lecture to lay audiences. When it had become clear that the Royal Institution was primarily a meeting-ground of the intelligentsia, and less committed to conveying science to the people than had been the intention of its founder, the British Association for the Advancement of Science was founded. In the 1860s the British Association organized lectures for working people by such distinguished scientists as T. H. Huxley. The annual meeting of the British Association is still one of the occasions when distinguished scientists and lay people can meet. The speed of the modern scientific enterprise has reached such a state where it is no longer fashionable, as was once the case, for distinguished scientists to announce the results of their work at meetings of the Royal Institution or of the British Association, but they still remain organizations of sufficient prestige to attract distinguished scientists out of their laboratories.

With the tremendous audiences which television, and to a lesser extent radio, command, it is not over-fanciful to hope that some arrangement may be achieved whereby as much prestige accrues to the popularization of science as to its furtherance through research.

8 *Science Culture*

THE social purpose of science is not to be found in science itself. Rather it is to be found in the use to which individuals and groups of individuals put the science they know. To be fully integrated in the general culture, science needs to be expressive and instrumental. That is to say, it must express in some fundamental way the reaction to environment of the groups using that science; and it must be instrumental in helping groups of people to achieve the social, political, economic, moral, and other objectives which they have set themselves. Culture, Peterkiewicz (1971) has written, is what you are prepared to defend. It follows that the science transmitted to young people through education and through broadcasting must meet some felt need.

As we have seen, it can be argued that much scientific activity meets the felt needs of only a small sector of the community, mainly professional scientists. The need it meets for them is that of 'international visibility', recognition as expert puzzle-solvers within their own discipline. The professionalization and bureaucratization of science, which produces this institutional pressure for prestige, has a cascade effect throughout the educational system. Nearly all professional scientists are socialized into their disciplines through universities. If the science-teaching activity of universities is aimed primarily at socializing those who are going to become professional scientists, to the neglect of those who do not intend to do so, it is inevitable that the effects will be felt throughout the system. It is an unavoidable social fact—sanctified by the Registrar-General's method of classifying the British population—that occupations are ranked with reference to each other in terms of prestige, not necessarily in terms of financial reward. The route towards occupations with prestige is through education, particularly through the universities.

The universities can lay down the paths—not only for scientists but also for students of other subjects—which are willingly or unwillingly followed by those seeking high qualifications and jobs carrying high prestige. Modification of curricula to effect an integration of science with general culture is therefore a social rather than a purely academic problem.

It is perhaps difficult to disentangle social activity from purely academic activity. Indeed, a social reorientation towards science can be achieved only through modification of curricula; and modification of curricula can be achieved only through primarily social measures. In terms of pure curriculum reform, the principal task seems to be to make the science curriculum relevant to the interests and needs of the present-day pupils.

It is important to note that in this respect the expressive qualities of science as an item of culture are probably more important than the instrumental ones. It seems that young people are more interested in the expressive value of the subjects they study than in their instrumental value in securing for them a rapid route to prestige in employment. If young people were simply interested in getting into universities, they would most likely rush to take science A-levels. For example, MacAlhone (1969) showed that in 1969 92 per cent of candidates with passes in mathematics, physics, and chemistry got places at university. Sixth-form science pupils who did badly at G.C.E. A-level had four times as good a chance of getting into university as colleagues who had taken the arts. Nevertheless, there is a strong movement towards the taking of a mix of A-levels (which may not commend itself to universities) and an even stronger desire among those doing pure science or pure arts A-levels to take a mixture. This is known not only from the Schools Council Survey (1970) but also from an enquiry into the sixth form carried out by *New Sixth* (1969).

Seeking to diagnose the relative trend away from science, engineering, and technology, the Dainton Committee (Council for Scientific Policy 1968) suggested various possible reasons for this unpopularity. For example, they noted (p. 78) that the impact made on a student by his first contact with science in secondary school is crucially important, especially if it happens at about the time he is required to make curriculum decisions with career implications.

When science is unimaginative in presentation, and its essential qualities are shrouded in heavily factual content; when it seems far removed from human affairs and without roots in contemporary technological achievements such as space travel, or the transistor; when there is a body of received knowledge to be acquired before speculation and imagination can be given free rein; then curiosity and enthusiasm will surely be quenched.

The Dainton Committee suggested that there was an urgent need to look afresh at science curricula and that the ways in which curriculum reform and syllabus revision come about.

One of the reasons the Dainton Committee suggested for the lack of appeal in science and technology was that for many young people science, engineering, and technology seemed out of touch with human and social affairs (para. 151). They noted that it was significant that biological and medical studies had not suffered the decline of physical sciences; and part of the attraction of the social sciences is that they deal with people and with society. The objectivity of science and the purposefulness of technology had become identified for some pupils with insensitivity and indifference.

The crucial problem seems to be that of achieving social relevance in the science curriculum. As MacPherson (1968, p. 270) commented, discussing the Dainton Report, 'if science were compulsory it must be attractive; if it is not attractive, it will only suffer to be made compulsory; and if it were attractive, it would not need to be compulsory'.

There seems to be sufficient interest among pupils at school in a broadly based education for interestingly taught science not to have to be compulsory. The pressures tending to make science uninteresting are, as has been noted, social.

Before discussing the prestige problem of the 'international visibility, publish-or-perish' syndrome, it is worth reviewing briefly the constraints on curriculum objective discussed so far in this book and noting where change is possible.

(1) In *primary* education (see Chapter 3), the 'integrated day' would seem to hold high promise. Pupils not only have time to follow their interests without the pressure of public examinations; they also have the opportunity to adopt a 'scientific' approach to phenomena which is effectively undistinguished from every other approach which they may make. Although there is at present a severe shortage of teachers with scientific training, for those who have taken science there is an unparalleled opportunity in primary education for imaginative teaching which will introduce pupils to

the approach of the scientist. In primary education, therefore, the initiative lies with the individual schools.

(2) In teaching for the *Certificate of Secondary Education*, there are similar opportunities for a flexible and imaginative approach through the Mode III system of examining (see Chapter 4). Schools are able, under the scheme, to devise their own syllabus of science education based on local talent, local facilities, and local opportunities for study, and to have the syllabus examined by teachers at the school with outside moderation. Although, as was noted, there seems to be a disappointing reluctance to experiment with Mode III examining, the initiative once again lies with the individual schools.

(3) In the *General Certificate of Education O-level*, despite the vigorous efforts of the Nuffield Foundation, there still seems to be a tendency to teach primarily facts. Facts are easier to teach than ideas and conceptual understanding; and the danger (noted by Barnard and McCreath 1970) that O-levels are used as a pre-selecting device for university entry may tempt teachers to opt for 'safe' approaches to their subject-matter. However (as noted in Chapter 4), the examining boards who administer the examinations for the schools are essentially 'in business'. It is their task to examine what the schools teach, and, despite what may be the popular belief among teachers, examining boards are ready to modify their syllabuses when requested to do so. Once again, it seems, the initiative lies with the schools.

(4) In *Sixth-form education*, although many pupils are not intending to proceed to higher education, the pressure of university entry requirements is severely felt. There is clear evidence that these requirements determine what combinations of subjects a pupil will take. The content of individual A-level syllabuses can, of course, be modified by the examining boards in collaboration with the schools. But neither the schools nor the examining boards are going to take any drastic action until they are convinced that any new examinations they devise are likely to be accepted as 'currency' by universities. Although a sixth-form curriculum should cater for every type of interest, in practice administrative possibilities limit what can be done. For pupils wishing to specialize entirely in the arts or to specialize entirely in the sciences, present sixth-form provision would seem to be very good indeed. However, for the apparently growing proportion of sixth-formers who would like to take a mix of A-levels, the situation is daunting. There are, as has been argued,

very good cultural reasons why students majoring in the arts should be encouraged to maintain contact with science. However, the utilitarian argument will perhaps have more force: that is to say, if some pupils are being deterred from entering careers in science and technology through mistaken beliefs about what these subjects actually involve—perhaps in turn resulting from poor teaching at junior level—there is every reason to defer irrevocable choices to the last possible moment. As Judge has said (1969, p. 432), '... I would really argue ... for later choice on the basis that a later choice is bound to be a better-informed choice. If in the end everybody fled from science, then one would really have, with great sadness, to conclude that science *deserved* to be fled from!'

With the present competitive situation of university entry, it is perhaps unrealistic to expect pupils to take a mix of A-levels when universities do not seem to encourage this. It is equally unrealistic to expect pupils to take science as a minority study if they get no credit for what they do. The very rapid expansion of General Studies A-levels is, therefore, a development to be applauded.

(5) The greatest contribution which *universities* could make to science culture would be to modify their entry requirements. There is a widespread belief that to involve oneself with a 'discipline' one must study a great deal of one subject. This is to equate depth with quantity. Perhaps the most pernicious objective of university single-discipline courses is to attempt to 'cover the ground'. In a given subject, it is clearly possible for a student studying at university for three years to learn only a minute fraction of what is known. Assuming, for the sake of argument, that it was possible for a student to 'cover' 2 per cent of everything that was known in his subject, say history, in his time at university, would anything be lost if he only attempted to cover 1 per cent? Assuming he had learned how to study, and assuming that the university made it clear that education is a life process, the pressure to 'cover the ground' might be seen to be what it is—the abnegation of the university's responsibility to sort wheat from chaff.

There are undoubted pressures on students and staff alike resulting from the British pattern of a three-year first degree. The beneficial effects of an additional year are clearly seen in the opportunities afforded to students of the University of Keele. Granted that university courses of three years' duration are not accepted in any profession as complete training, and granted that some sort of post-graduate study or professional training is required after the degree, might it not be sensible to let those who wished to study a subject to an advanced level of scholarship stay on to do the now common one-year postgraduate master's course or, in special cases, the three-year doctorate? The Pippard scheme (1969), which proposes a two-year first degree would, in effect, simply reduce the length—and therefore the quality—of university experience for many students, without really solving the problem of broadening the universities' educational programme.

In view of the ethos of universities, with the heavy emphasis on scholarship, it is a little unrealistic to expect drastic changes in university teaching designed to broaden a student's education into disciplines other than the one for which he is registered. For those with the stamina and intellectual resilience, joint honours courses may provide a satisfactory method of achieving a broad education. However, from what one can gather, the process of integration is usually left to the student, and it is a process which is often intellectually extremely taxing. One views with dismay the path to general education in universities: a path often strewn with good intentions which have come to grief through failure to acknowledge the powerful tendency of universities to divide into specialist departments.

Senior members of university departments are likely to be scholars identified more with the international structure of their discipline than with the institutional structure of their university. (There are, of course, exceptions to every rule, and particularly when a group of distinguished scholars have the opportunity to found a new university and to write a new syllabus.) Young scholars, particularly those seeking tenure, fresh from research, are probably the least likely to be interested in furthering the general education of their students, but once again, there will be exceptions. One possibility is to offer students the opportunity to do a piece of work, and possibly write a dissertation, on a subject chosen by them in a field outside the one in which they are majoring. Given suitable school education, an intelligent student does not need 'teaching' in the sense of 'instruction'; rather, he needs the use of a good library and the guidance of someone who will, from time to time, question him about what he is doing. To set up such a scheme, all that would be required would be a series of proposed dissertation topics from which students could choose, or the opportunity for students to propose their own topics, and occasional supervision. One advantage of such a scheme is that the topics for dissertations could be chosen in relation to the research interests of teaching staff in faculties other than those for which students were registered for their majors. Provided that endeavour in the field outside one's major was adequately rewarded with marks or, perhaps, 'credits' (see Elton 1968), students who had from their schooling achieved an interest in science could continue to pursue it with minimum inconvenience to their home departments.

Prospective employers of university graduates could, of course, do a great deal to foster the science education of non-scientists by asking, in interviews and in testimonials, for some evidence of work of this sort.

(6) *Broadcasting* is regarded, especially by television viewers, as relaxation. It is neither possible nor politically desirable to force science on an unwilling public. Kriegbaum (1968, p. 55) has emphasized the value of television for generating general awareness. But, as Wade and Schramm (1969) have shown, newspapers and journals are used more than television as sources of public knowledge of science. Again, better-educated persons are more likely than others to seek science information from more than one source, and the more education a person has, the more likely he is to use print as his major source of news and information. A corollary of this is that the choice of print as a major source is likely to bring with it more knowledge and deeper knowledge—at least in the areas of science and health. One cannot, of course, 'go back over' a difficult part of a broadcast. It is likely that those who are genuinely interested in science will look to books and journals for the information they want.

A greater infusion of science into broadcasting will probably be an effect of the spread of science culture, not a cause of it. However, there may be an important lesson to be learned from the science programmes which seem to have greatest popularity. The British public seems to have a passion for medical programmes; that is to say programmes which relate science to their immediate, felt, personal needs. The lesson may be that if science is to become part of general culture it must be seen to be socially relevant.

Provided that the social relevance of the subject can be clearly demonstrated, there are clear educational advantages to be gained

L

from the exposure of non-scientists to the practices and preoccupations of the physical sciences. The earlier a pupil can be given direct experience of formulating hypotheses, testing them by measurement, and so on, the more likely he is to develop a favourable attitude to science.

A great deal of physical science relies upon the shorthand of mathematics. Indeed, as Brookes (1959) has argued, the language of a science, even of a science in an early stage of development, will already have become a limited field of discourse in which the propositions depend upon and support each other. A proposition abstracted from a scientific discourse can be interpreted as a scientific statement within this unity only by someone familiar with the whole field of discourse. If this view is correct, then there can be no short cut to understanding science. The theoretical terms of a science are not simply a list of labels, except to the non-scientist. To the scientist, they are summations of his scientific experience, not substitutes for it. That is to say, a non-scientist might ask of a scientist, 'What are you doing and why are you doing it?' and expect to get intelligible replies; he could not, however, go to the important next stage, that is, to ask '*How* are you doing it?'—for the reply he would receive, if it were not to travesty the truth, would rely on a sophisticated form of shorthand, probably involving mathematics. In short, there may be many areas of physical science which are simply not available to students who are unwilling, or unable, to absorb the whole of the language of the discipline.

Again, it may well be true, as argued by Hudson (1960, 1963, 1966), that there are differences of personality and differences of aptitude among students, and that some are simply not at home in what he calls 'convergent' thinking. It is unlikely that an individual will be imbued with science culture against his will, particularly if he is constitutionally antipathetic towards it.

For some students, involvement with science culture may well be best achieved through involvement with *technology*. The objectives of science and of technology are fundamentally different. The objective of science can be described (at the risk of oversimplification) as systematic description; the objective of technology is the systematic extension of human faculties. Both are obviously programmatic, but technology is a form of social science. That is to say, the specifications for a technological device or system arise directly from some economic, social, political, or other human need. But, the *operational* similarity of science and technology has already been noted. This may, indeed, be its very strength.

Already, there is vigorous activity in offering technology in the schools—see, for example, Schools Council Working Paper No. 18, *Technology and the Schools* (1968) and also D. T. Kelly (1969*a*, 1969*b*). One of the advantages of the approach to science through technology is that it can be achieved at practically any level of academic achievement. There is an impressive selection of descriptions and case-histories of applied science projects and investigations in *School Science and Technology* (Schools Council 1969). For example, there is a report (pp. 180f.) of how some young students, apparently resistant to learning science subjects, became interested in the manufacture of cosmetics. Their study involved an interesting mixture of science, technology, and social science. In chemistry they studied waxes, oils, emulsions, water supply, etc.; in biology they studied physiology, skin, digestion, hair, hygiene, etc.; in physics they studied the physical properties of materials, light, and colour; in geography they studied the origin of the raw materials they used; in sociology they studied the social history of hygiene and the use of cosmetics, and advertising psychology and consumer research. All these studies focused on the fabrication of some cosmetics, and this proved effective in generating interest among girls.

Sensitively handled, the approach to science culture through the medium of technology could, in principle, meet all of the major objectives of science education proposed in Chapter 2: clearly, science and practical problems are related. Secondly, the demystification of science is achieved by students undertaking small-scale scientific investigations. Thirdly, it might be hoped, the ethics of observation would be learned by the necessity of testing claims to knowledge. Fourthly, it should not be difficult to show the imaginatively satisfying order achieved by scientific description through a carefully selected investigation of phenomena. Finally, through technology, students could be introduced to certain major phenomena and ideas.

A subsidiary benefit to be derived from this approach might be the refurbishing of the image not only of scientists but also of technologists. If the image of scientists can, from time to time, become blighted, so too can that of technologists, as Hutchings has shown (Hutchings 1963, Hutchings and Heyworth 1963).

At university level, it might be possible for arts or social science students to take part jointly with engineers in technological projects. It is not uncommon for engineering students to receive instruction in social sciences as part of their degree courses. For example, at the Imperial College of Science and Technology, electrical engineering students have, for some years, undertaken group projects under the guidance of members of the engineering staff in which they have investigated engineering questions which are complicated by economic, political, and social factors, or have studied social and economic questions which are of interest and importance to the engineering profession. Students have studied such subjects as the possible uses of television for education in India and Ghana; the likely effects upon the electricity industry of the discovery of gas in the North Sea; the economic and social effects of the progress of automation in selected sectors of British industry; the automatic control of civil aircraft in Europe; the implications of the introduction of the metric system for the electrical engineering industries; the choice of product for a new electrical engineering factory to be set up overseas; medical technology and the law. Students have even carried out project work in developing countries (see Goodlad 1970, Brown and Goodlad 1971). There is no reason why such projects should not be carried out jointly by students of engineering and students of the humanities or social sciences.

One benefit of such projects is that they can in theory, like dissertations, be related in some way to the research interests of the university teaching staff. By taking part in joint projects, arts students might learn what could be measured by the techniques of the physical sciences, and engineering students could learn where the techniques of physical sciences stopped and where the skills of lawyer, sociologist, geographer, and anthropologist came to bear. As with dissertations, suitable rewards would have to be devised for students who took part. In like manner, some positive encouragement might have to be given to university staff-members supervising such projects so that they did not suffer in the academic marketplace.

But if science culture is to become a reality, more will be needed than tinkering with curricula, or the reform of entry requirements by the universities. The basic problem comes down to the prestige system of scientific disciplines. This is the fundamental social phenomenon which currently inhibits all well-meaning attempts to infuse general culture with science. If scientific activity is to enjoy a favourable climate of public opinion, positive steps must be taken to achieve that climate. At present, as noted in Chapter 7, the honours go to those who advance knowledge and not to those who disseminate it. If it is indeed true that science and technology are symbiotic, and if the economic health of the nation depends upon technology, there would seem to be a very strong case for fabricating a prestige system which recognizes achievement in the popularization of science. It would be comparatively easy for civil Honours to be awarded for services to science education. What would, however, have a much more far-reaching effect would be for the Royal Society to elect Fellows for service to the community in popularizing science as well as for brilliance in scientific discovery.

Some of the most effective popularizers of science are already Fellows of the Royal Society, but they have been elected to that august body for their *science* rather than for *popularizing* it. If the crowning glory of a Fellowship of the Royal Society could be awarded for service to science—either through popularization or through political activity, or through any other similar work—there can be little doubt that science would rapidly become part of general culture. Once that had been achieved, the question 'Science for what?' might ultimately become irrelevant. With vigorous science education for non-specialists at all stages of the educational system, it might be hoped that science would become an accepted part of expressive culture (as a form of self-knowledge) and a potent part of instrumental culture (as informed, confident, question-asking).

Bibliography

ADAMS, M. (1959) Medicine through television. *World Press News 13*, February 1959.
ADVISORY COUNCIL ON SCIENTIFIC POLICY (1960) *Annual Report 1959-60.* H.M.S.O.
AMOS, R. (1968) Teachers' opinions on the place of the scientific method in biology courses. *British Journal of Educational Psychology 38*, 323.
ASHBY, E. (1966) *Technology and the academics.* Macmillan, London.
ASSOCIATION FOR SCIENCE EDUCATION (1963) *Science in sixth-form general education.* John Murray, London.
ASSOCIATION OF COMMONWEALTH UNIVERSITIES (1963) for the Committee of Vice-Chancellors and Principals of the Universities of the United Kingdom. *A compendium of university entrance requirements.* Annually since 1963.
ASSOCIATION OF UNIVERSITIES OF THE BRITISH COMMONWEALTH (1960) *Proceedings of the Home Universities Conference: The future of the general degree.*
BAGRIT, L. (1965) *The Age of Automation: the BBC Reith lectures 1964.* Weidenfeld and Nicolson, London.
BAINBRIDGE, J. (ed.) (1969) *Experience, experiment and explain. A survey of Nuffield Science trials in Northumberland 1963-8.* Northumberland Education Committee.
BAKER, J. R. (1967) *Science in sixth-form general studies.* Occasional publication of the General Studies Association No. L/13/67.
—— (1969) Survey of attitudes to general studies science. *School Science Review,* September 1969, Curriculum Development Section, pp. 176-83.
—— (1970) A survey of the position of general studies science. *Bulletin of the General Studies Association 15,* pp. 22-38.
BARNARD, G. A. *and* McCREATH, M. D. (1970) Subject commitments and the demand for higher education. *Journal of the Royal Statistical Society 133,* 358-93.
BARZUN, J. (1954) *Teaching in America.* Doubleday Anchor, New York.
BASSEY, M. (1963) *School science for tomorrow's citizens.* Pergamon Press, Oxford.
BELL, DANIEL (1966) *The reforming of general education. The Columbia College experience in its national setting.* Columbia University Press.
BELSON, W. A. (1967) *The impact of television.* Crosby Lockwood, London.
BERNAL, J. D. (1954) *Science in history.* C. A. Watts, London.
BERNSTEIN, B. (1971) On the classification and framing of educational know-

ledge. In M. Young (ed.), *Knowledge and Control*, pp. 47–69. Collier-Macmillan, London.
BEST, E. (1955) Can school science be educative, teaching the habit of engineering? *Times Educational Supplement* 18 February 1955, No. 2077, p. 167.
BLOOM, B. S. *et al.* (1956) *Taxonomy of educational objectives. The Classification of Educational Goals. Handbook 1: Cognitive Domain.* Longmans, London.
BOARD OF EDUCATION (1938) *Report of the Consultative Committee on Secondary Education, with special reference to grammar schools and technical high schools.* (The Spens Report). H.M.S.O., London.
BRADBURY, F. R. (ed.) (1969) *Words and numbers: A students' guide to intellectual methods.* Edinburgh University Press.
BRADSHAW, K. D. (1966) A school reaction to CSE. *Forum 9*, pp. 28–30.
BRIDGHAM, R. G. (1969) Conceptions of science and learning science. *School Review*, November 1969, No. 78, pp. 25–40.
BRIERLEY, J. K. (1960) Some science for arts sixth-forms. *School Science Review*, November 1969, No. 42, pp. 85–102.
BRISTOL UNIVERSITY (1968) *A joint university–schools proposal for the revision of sixth-form curricula and examinations.* Bristol.
BRITISH ASSOCIATION FOR THE ADVANCEMENT OF SCIENCE (1933) *General science in schools.* British Association, London.
—— (1961) *The place of science in the primary school.* British Association, London.
BRITISH BROADCASTING CORPORATION (1970) *Audience research in the United Kingdom.* BBC Publications, London.
BROOKES, B. C. (1959) The difficulty of interpreting science. *The Listener 62*, 519–21.
BROWN, J. and GOODLAD, J. S. R. (1971) Grassroots engineering. *Electronics and Power*, February 1971, pp. 49–53.
CALDER, R. (1964) Common understanding of science. *Impact of Science on Society 14*, 179–95.
CAMPBELL, M. B. (1966) *Nonspecialist study in the undergraduate curricula of the New Universities and Colleges of Advanced Technology in England.* University of Michigan Comparative Education Dissertation Series, No. 10.
CAPLOW, T. and McGEE, R. J. (1958) *The academic marketplace.* Basic Books, New York and Anchor Books, New York 1965.
CASEY, C. (1968) Educational Objectives of sixth-form general studies, vols. 1 and 2. Ph.D. Dissertation, University of Manchester.
CENTRAL ADVISORY COUNCIL FOR EDUCATION (ENGLAND), Ministry of Education (1959) *15 to 18.* (The Crowther Report). H.M.S.O., London.
—— (1963) *Half our future.* (The Newsom Report). H.M.S.O., London.
CENTRAL ADVISORY COUNCIL FOR EDUCATION, DEPARTMENT OF EDUCATION AND SCIENCE (1967) *Children and their primary schools* (The Plowden Report). H.M.S.O., London.
CENTRAL STATISTICAL OFFICE (1971) *Annual Abstract of Statistics* No. 108, H.M.S.O., London.
CLOW, A. (1956) Presentation of Science to the public. *Journal of the Royal Institute of Chemistry 80*, 437.
COHEN, I. B. and WATSON, F. G. (eds) (1952) *General education in science.* Harvard University Press, Cambridge, Mass.
COMMITTEE ON HIGHER EDUCATION, MINISTRY OF EDUCATION (1963) *Higher education.* (The Robbins Report). Cmnd. 2154, H.M.S.O., London.

COMMITTEE ON MANPOWER RESOURCES FOR SCIENCE AND TECHNOLOGY, DEPARTMENT OF EDUCATION AND SCIENCE (1968) *The flow into employment of scientists, engineers and technologists.* (The Swann Report). Report of the working group on manpower for scientific growth. Cmnd. 3760, H.M.S.O., London.

CONANT, J. B. (1946) The scientific education of the layman. *Yale Review 36,* 15–36.

—— (1951) *On understanding science* (2nd edn). Mentor Books, New York.

—— (ed.) (1957) *Harvard case histories in experimental science,* Vols. 1 and 2. Harvard University Press, Cambridge, Mass.

COUNCIL FOR SCIENTIFIC POLICY, DEPARTMENT OF EDUCATION AND SCIENCE (1968) *Enquiry into the flow of candidates in science and technology into higher education.* (The Dainton Report). Cmnd. 3541, H.M.S.O., London.

CROSS, M. *and* JOBLING, R. G. (1969) The English new universities—a preliminary enquiry. *Universities Quarterly* spring 1969, pp. 173–82.

DAICHES, D. (1963) The university curriculum and the idea of the unity of knowledge. *Advancement of Science* July 1963, pp. 128–32.

—— (ed.) (1964) *The idea of a new university.* André Deutsch, London.

DAVIS, R. C. (1958) *The public impact of science in the mass media. A report on a nation-wide survey for the National Association of Science Writers.* University of Michigan, Survey Research Centre, Institute for Social Research.

DEPARTMENT OF EDUCATION AND SCIENCE (1961) *Science in primary schools.* Educational Pamphlet No. 42. H.M.S.O., London.

—— (1969) *Reports on education,* May, 1969.

DUPREE, A. HUNTER (1961) Public education for science and technology. *Science* 134, 716–18.

EAST ANGLIAN EXAMINING BOARD (1969) *Examination papers for 1969.*

ELTON, L. R. B. (1968) The assessment of students—a new approach. *Universities Quarterly 22,* 291–301.

EPSTEIN, H. J. (1970) *A strategy for education.* Oxford University Press, Oxford and New York.

GERBNER, G. (1969) Institutional pressures upon mass communicators. *Sociological Review, Monograph* No. 13, pp. 205–48. University of Keele.

GILL, N. M. (1969) Integrated studies in the B.Ed. course. *Universities Quarterly 24,* 195–20.

GOODLAD, J. S. R. (1970) Project work in developing countries: A British experiment in engineering education. *International Journal of Electrical Engineering Education 8,* 135–40.

GREENAWAY, F. (1958) Notes towards the definition of a scientific culture. *Universities Quarterly 13,* 23–33.

GREGORY, R. (1922) *Report of the British Association* 1922, p. 207.

GRESSWELL, B. (1970) Science for all—a new look. *School Science Review 51,* 528–33.

HALSEY, A. H. *and* TROW, M. A. (1971) *The British academics.* Faber, London.

HARVARD COMMITTEE (1945) *General education in a free society.* Harvard University Press, Cambridge, Mass.

HOAGLAND, H. (1960) Science and the new humanism. *Science 143,* 111–14.

HOLTON, G. (1960) Modern science and the intellectual tradition. *Science 131,* 1187–93.

—— (1963) Science for non-scientists: criteria for college programs. *Teachers College Record 64,* 497–509.

HOOD, S. (1967) *A survey of television.* Heinemann, London.

HUDSON, L. (1960) A differential test of arts/science aptitude. *Nature, Lond. 186*, 413–14.

—— (1963) Personality and scientific aptitude. *Nature*, Lond. *198*, 913–14.

—— *Contrary imaginations.* Pelican Books, Harmondsworth.

HUTCHINGS, D. W. (1963) Sixth-form scientists in search of an image. *Universities Quarterly 17*, 254–9.

—— and HEYWORTH, P. (1963) *Technology and the sixth-form boy.* Oxford University Department of Education.

ILIFFE, A. H. (1968) *The foundation year in the University of Keele.* University of Keele.

INGRAM, D. J. E. (1966) Physics at Keele. *Physics Education 1*, 254–64.

JAMES, E. (1949) Specialisation and general education in the sixth-form. *Universities Quarterly 3*, 672–8.

JAMES, W. S. (1957) The slump in science teaching. *New Scientist* 19 September 1957, pp. 15–17.

JENKINS, E. W. (1967) The attitude of teachers to the introduction of Nuffield Chemistry. *School Science Review 167*, 231–42.

JEVONS, F. R. (1969*a*) *The teaching of science.* Allen and Unwin, London.

—— (1969*b*) Science outside the laboratory. *Universities Quarterly 23*, 397–408.

JOHNSON, K. G. (1961) Differential judgements of science news stories and their structural correlates. Ph.D. dissertation, University of Wisconsin.

JUDGE, H. G. (1969) The crisis in science teaching in schools. *Journal of the Royal Society of Arts 117*, 425–35.

KELLY, D. T. (1969*a*) Technology in the sixth-form. *School Science Review 51*, 270–81.

—— (1969*b*) Project technology. *School Science Review 50*, 720–33.

KELLY, P. (1967) Trends in biological education—an international review. *Journal of Biological Education 1*, 1–12.

—— (1969) Curriculum. *Education and training 11*, 503–4.

KERR, J. F. (1964) *Practical work in science. An account of an enquiry sponsored by the Gulbenkian Foundation into the nature and purpose of practical work in school science teaching in England and Wales.* Leicester University Press.

KRATHWOHL, D. R., BLOOM, B. S., and MASIA, B. B. (1956) *Taxonomy of educational objectives, The classification of educational goals. Handbook 2: Affective Domain.* Longmans, London.

KRIEGBAUM, H. (1968) *Science and the mass media.* University of London Press.

KUHN, T. S. (1970) *The structure of scientific revolutions.* (2nd edn.) University of Chicago Press, 1962.

KUSLAN, L. I. and STONE, I. H. (1968) *Teaching children science—an enquiry approach.* Wadsworth, Belmont, California.

LEE, D. (1970) QFOAS and all that. *Conference 7*, 32–4.

LEEDS UNIVERSITY INSTITUTE OF EDUCATION (1968) *CSE—an assessment of progress. Proceedings of a conference held at the University of Leeds, May 1968.*

LEWIS, D. G. (1965) Objectives in the teaching of science. *Educational Research 7*, 186–9.

LEWIS, J. (1965) The Nuffield Physics Project. *Bulletin of the Institute of Physics and the Physical Society 16*, 81–94.

LORD, M. A. and RITCHIE, W. R. (1962) The American Physical Science Study

164   *Bibliography*

Committee Course. *Bulletin of the Institute of Physics and the Physical Society 13*, 3–5.
MACALHONE, B. (1969) The A level stakes. *Where 45*, 136–7.
MCCLOY, J. (1956) The presentation of science: television. *Journal of the Royal Institute of Chemistry 80*, 447–9.
MCGRATH, E. J. (1948) *Towards general education*. Macmillan, New York.
MCPHERSON, A. (1968) The Dainton Report—A Scottish dissent. *Universities Quarterly 22*, 254–73.
MEAD, M. and MÉTRAUX, R. (1957) Image of the scientist among high school students. *Science 126*, 384–90.
MEDAWAR, P. B. (1967) *The art of the soluble*. Methuen, London.
—— (1969) *Induction and intuition in scientific thought*. Methuen, London.
MINISTRY OF EDUCATION (1943) *Curriculum and examinations in secondary schools*. (The Norwood Report). H.M.S.O., London.
—— (1960a) *Secondary school examination other than the General Certificate of Education. Report of a Committee appointed by the SSEC in July 1958.* (The Beloe Report). H.M.S.O., London.
—— (1960b) *Science in secondary schools*. Pamphlet 38. H.M.S.O., London.
—— (1963) *Scope and standards of the Certificate of Secondary Education.* 7th Report of the SSEC. H.M.S.O., London.
NAGEL, E. (1959) The place of science in a liberal education. *Daedalus 88*, 56–74.
NATIONAL FROEBEL FOUNDATION (1966) *Children learning through scientific interests.*
NEVILLE, P. (1968) No place for absolute truths. *School Science Review 49*, 859–67.
NEWBOLD, D. E. (1969) Student understanding of science and scientists. An enquiry into general scientific education in sixth forms. B. Litt. Dissertation, University of Oxford.
NEW SIXTH *Enquiry into the sixth form. New Sixth 2, 5.*
NOWELL-SMITH, P. (1958) *Education in a university*. Leicester University Press.
NYHOLM, R. S. (1964) Education in science—for whom and for what purpose? Marchon Lecture, University of Newcastle upon Tyne.
OLIVER, R. A. C. (1961) *General studies (advanced) 1960*. Joint Matriculation Board, Manchester.
—— (1965) History and philosophy of science in the JMB General Studies examination. *Bulletin of the General Studies Association 6*, 30–3.
—— and LEWIS, D. G. (1970) Elements in sixth-form general studies. *Journal of Curriculum Studies 2*, 162–74.
ORGANISATION FOR ECONOMIC CO-OPERATION AND DEVELOPMENT (1963) *Science and the policies of governments. The implications of science and technology for national and international affairs.*
OXFORD DELEGACY OF LOCAL EXAMINATIONS. *General report 1968–9.*
OXFORD UNIVERSITY (1969) *The proposed Honours School in human sciences. Oxford University Gazette 99*, 1438–40.
PASKE, G. H. (1967) Science for humanists. *Liberal Education Bulletin of the American Colleges* May 1967, pp. 252–63.
PETERKIEWICZ, J. (1971) Trust the trees. *Times Literary Supplement* 30 July 1971, p. 909.
PETERSON, A. D. C. (1960a) *Arts and science sides in the sixth form*. Oxford University Department of Education and Gulbenkian Foundation, Oxford.

PETERSON, A. D. C. (1960*b*) The myth of subject-mindedness. *Universities Quarterly 14*, 223–32.

PIPPARD, A. B. (1969) The educated scientist. *Physics Bulletin 20*, 453–9.

RALLISON, R. (1946) The scientific interests of children. *Discovery 7*, 51–4.

REID, R. W. (1969) Television producer and scientist. *Nature, Lond. 223*, 455–8.

REIF, F. (1969) Science education for non-science students. *Science 164*, 1032–7.

RUDD, W. G. A. (1968) The North West Regional Curriculum Development Project. *Forum 10*, 40–2.

SCHOOLS COUNCIL (SSEC) (1963) The certificate of Secondary Education. *Examinations Bulletin* No. 1. H.M.S.O., London.

—— (1965) *Science and the young school leaver. Working Paper* No. 1.

—— (1966*a*) *Mathematics in primary schools. Curriculum Bulletin* No. 1.

—— (1966*b*) *Science in the sixth form. Working Paper* No. 4.

—— (1966*c*) *Sixth form curriculum and examinations. Working Paper* No. 5.

—— (1967) *Some further proposals for sixth-form work. Working Paper* No. 16.

—— (1968) *Technology and the schools. Working Paper* No. 18.

—— (1969*a*) *School science and technology. Selected descriptions and case histories of applied science projects and investigations.* (Edited by D. T. Kelly.) Schools Council, London.

—— (1969*b*) *The middle years of school. From 8–13. Working Paper* No. 22.

——(1969*c*) *General studies 16–18. Working Paper* No. 25. Evans/Methuen, London.

—— (1969*d*) Science: Nuffield and the Schools Council. *Dialogue 4*, 12.

—— (1970) *Sixth Form Survey.* Vol. 1. *Sixth form pupils and teachers.* Books for Schools.

—— (1971) *A common system of examining at 16 plus. Examinations Bulletin* 23, Evans/Methuen, London.

SCHRAMM, W. (1962) *Science and the public mind. Miscellaneous Publication* No. 62.3. American Association for the Advancement of Science.

SCIENCE MASTERS' ASSOCIATION (1950) *Report on the teaching of general science.* John Murray, London.

SCUPHAM, J. (1967) *Broadcasting and the community.* C. A. Watts, London.

SECONDARY SCHOOLS EXAMINATION COUNCIL (1963) *The Certificate of Secondary Education: some suggestions for teachers and examiners. Examinations Bulletin* No. 1. H.M.S.O., London.

SIBSON, R. (1969) Examinations—the second estate. *Dialogue 3*, 12–13.

SILVEY, R. J. (1962) Because it's free. *Contrast* spring 1962.

SINGER, A. (1966) *Science broadcasting.* BBC Publications, London.

SMITH, HUSTON (ed.) (1955) *The purposes of higher education.* Harper Bros., New York.

SNOW, C. P. (1964) *The two cultures: and a second look.* Cambridge University Press.

SOUTH WESTERN EXAMINATIONS BOARD (1966) *Second Annual Report.* Bristol.

STANDING CONFERENCE ON UNIVERSITY ENTRANCE AND THE SCHOOLS COUNCIL JOINT WORKING PARTY ON SIXTH FORM CURRICULUM AND EXAMINATIONS (1969) *Proposals for the curriculum and examinations—a joint statement.*

SWALLOW, N. (1966) *Factual television.* Focal Press, London.

TANNENBAUM, P. H. (1969) The communication of scientific information. *Science 140*, 579.

TOULMIN, S. (1963) Science and our intellectual tradition. *Advancement of Science 20,* 28–34.

TRICKER, R. A. R. (1967) *The contribution of science to education.* Mills and Boon, London.

TROW, M. (1965) The idea of a new university. *Universities Quarterly 19,* 162–72.

UNIVERSITY GRANTS COMMITTEE (1958) *University development report 1952–57.* Cmnd. 534. H.M.S.O., London.

—— (1964) *University development 1957–62.* Cmnd. 2267, H.M.S.O., London.

URQUHART, D. J. (1970) Storage and retrieval of scientific information. *Times Literary Supplement* 3558, 519–20.

WADE, S. *and* SCHRAMM, W. (1969) The mass media as sources of public affairs, science, and health knowledge. *Public Opinion Quarterly 33* (2), 197–209.

WARREN, J. W. (1961) Errors in textbooks and the tradition of physics teaching. *Bulletin of the Institute of Physics and the Physical Society 12,* 309–13.

WEAVER, W. (1957) Science and the citizen. *Bulletin of the Atomic Scientists* 13 December 1957, pp. 361–5.

—— (1966) Why is it so important that science be understood? *Impact of Science on Society 16,* 41–50.

WEDELL, E. G. (1968) *Broadcasting and public policy.* Michael Joseph, London.

WEST YORKSHIRE AND LINDSEY REGIONAL EXAMINING BOARD (n.d.) *Information to parents about CSE.*

WHALLEY, G. E. (1969) *The Certificate of Secondary Education.* University of Leeds Institute of Education Paper No. 9.

WILLIAMS, R. (1968) *Communications* (revised edition). Penguin Books, Harmondsworth.

WRIGHT, C. R. (1960) Functional analysis and mass communication. *Public Opinion Quarterly 24* (4), 605–20.

YUDKIN, M. (ed.) (1969) *General education. A symposium on the teaching of non-specialists.* Allen Lane, the Penguin Press, Harmondsworth.

ZIMAN, J. M. (1968) *Public knowledge.* Cambridge University Press.

ZUCKERMAN, S. (1970) *Beyond the ivory tower. The frontiers of public and private science,* Weidenfeld and Nicolson, London.

Index of names

Adams, M., 141
Amos, R., 68
Ashby, E., 118
Association for Science Education, 99–100; *see also* Science Masters' Association
Association of Commonwealth Universities, 110–11, 116

Bagrit, L., 119
Bainbridge, J., 72–3
Baker, J. R., 101–4
Barnard, G. A., 46, 81, 152
Barzun, J., 36
Bassey, M., 66, 71
Bell, D., 108
Beloe Committee, *see* Ministry of Education
Belson, W. A., 4, 146
Bernal, J. D., 7–9, 13
Bernstein, B., 114–16, 124, 133
Best, E., 69
Bloom, B. S., 31–3, 60
Board of Education, 58
Bradbury, F. R., 125
Bradshaw, K. D., 64
Bridgham, R. G., 14
Brierley, J. K., 73
Bristol University, 84–5, 96, 107
British Association, 50, 67
British Broadcasting Corporation, 146
Brookes, B. C., 156
Brown, J., 158

Calder, R., 23
Campbell, M. B., 116
Caplow, T., 112–14, 133
Casey, C., 100–1

Central Advisory Council for Education (England), 46, 49, 55, 69, 75, 88–90
Central Statistical Office, 2
Clow, A., 145
Cohen, I. B., 69
Committee on Higher Education, 46, 109–12, 129
Committee on Manpower Resources for Science and Technology, 111, 134
Conant, J. B., 27, 36–8
Council for Scientific Policy, 47, 82–3, 110, 134, 150–1
Crowther Committee, *see* Central Advisory Council for Education (England)

Daiches, D., 116, 130
Dainton Committee, *see* Council for Scientific Policy
Davis, R. C., 143, 146
Department of Education and Science, 51–3, 54, 78
Dupree, A. Hunter, 23

Elton, L. R. B., 135–6, 152
Epstein, H. J., 41

Gerbner, G., 140
Gill, N. M., 78
Goodlad, J. S. R., 158
Greenaway, F., 18–19
Gregory, R., 66
Gresswell, B., 68

Halsey, A. H., 113–14
Harvard Committee, 108
Heywood, J., 120

Science for non-scientists